Teaching Young Language Learners

Also published in
Oxford Handbooks for Language Teachers

Teaching Young
Language Learners

Annamaria Pinter

OXFORD
UNIVERSITY PRESS

OXFORD
UNIVERSITY PRESS

Great Clarendon Street, Oxford OX2 6DP

Oxford University Press is a department of the University of Oxford.
It furthers the University's objective of excellence in research, scholarship,
and education by publishing worldwide in

Oxford New York

Auckland Cape Town Dar es Salaam Hong Kong Karachi
Kuala Lumpur Madrid Melbourne Mexico City Nairobi
New Delhi Shanghai Taipei Toronto

With offices in

Argentina Austria Brazil Chile Czech Republic France Greece
Guatemala Hungary Italy Japan Poland Portugal Singapore
South Korea Switzerland Thailand Turkey Ukraine Vietnam

OXFORD and OXFORD ENGLISH are registered trade marks of
Oxford University Press in the UK and in certain other countries

ISBN: 978 0 19 442207 9

Printed in China

This book is printed on paper from certified and well-managed sources.

To Keith and Thomas

CONTENTS

ACKNOWLEDGEMENTS

I would like to thank my colleagues Ema Ushioda and Shelagh Rixon, and all the anonymous readers for their invaluable feedback on previous drafts. My thanks also go to Julia Sallabank for her unfailing support and guidance during the writing process.

The authors and publisher are grateful to the following for permission to reprint copyright material:

Svetlana Azarova, Elena Ermolaeva, Eleonora Druzhinina, and Titul Publishers for permission to use the rhyme 'I eat apples' originally published in *Millie* 2: *Pupil's book* (page 97: exercise 3).

Cambridge University Press for permission to reproduce 'Nico and I Can Make…' taken from *Primary Colours Pupil's Book Starter*, an extract from 'King Cat's Corner' from *Primary Colours Pupil's Book 1* copyright © Cambridge University Press 2002, and 'Project Work: The monster with two sides' from *Primary Colours Pupil's Book 3* by D. Hicks and A. Littlejohn, copyright © Cambridge University Press 2003, reprinted by permission of the author and publisher.

CILT, the National Centre for Languages, for permission to reproduce two extracts from *My Languages Portfolio: European Language Portfolio – Junior version*, copyright © CILT, the National Centre for Languages, 2001.

Chris Fairclough Worldwide for a photo of a boy published in *Tip Top 4* by Shelagh Rixon (Macmillan, 1993)

David Higham Associates for the poem 'Cats Sleep Anywhere' by Eleanor Farjeon taken from *Blackbird Has Spoken* (Macmillan's Children's Book, 2000), copyright © Eleanor Farjeon 2000.

Macmillan Education for permission to reproduce 'Play with the paper street' from *Superworld Pupil's Book 2* written by Carol Read and Ana Soberón (Macmillan Education, 2000), 'Syllabus overview' from *Story Magic 1 Teacher's Book* by Susan House and Katherine Scott (Macmillan Education, 2003), 'The Giant's Causeway' from *Story Magic Pupil's Book 3* by Susan House and Katherine Scott (Macmillan Education, 2003), and 'Fact file: Traveller's guide' (text only) taken from *Story Magic Pupil's Book 3* (Macmillan Education, 2003), reprinted by permission of the publisher.

Oxford University Press for permission to reproduce 'Animals' from *Very Young Learners* by V. Reilly and S. M. Ward (Oxford University Press, 1997), 'Colour parsing' from *Young Learners* by S. Phillips (1993), 'How I like to learn

English' from *Assessing Young Learners* by S. Ioannou-Georgiou and P. Pavlou (2003), 'The Breakfast Show' from *Happy Street 2 Class Book* (2001), 'Listen and talk about your friend' from *Zabadoo 3 Class Book* by P. A. Davies (2002), all copyright © Oxford University Press and reprinted by permission of the publisher.

Seun Ju Park for permission to reproduce a questionnaire extract.

Pearson Education Limited for permission to reproduce a table on Gardner's Multiple Intelligences taken from *Child Development* by Laura E. Berk (Allyn and Bacon, Boston, MA, 2005), an extract from *Buzz 1 Teacher's Book* by J. Revell, P. Seligson, and J. Wright (BBC English, 1995), a Project from *New English Parade Starter B* by M. Herrera and T. Zanatta (Pearson Education Ltd, 2001), 'Student Oral Assessment Checklist' from *New English Parade Teacher's Book 1* by T. Zanatta and M. Herrera (Pearson Education Ltd, 2000), 'Listen to the radio programme' and 'Think and write' from *New English Parade 6* by M. Herrera and T. Zanatta (Pearson Education, 2001), all copyright © Pearson Education 2005, 'Think and Listen' and 'Boris the Second' from *Tip Top 4* by S. Rixon (Macmillan Publishers, 1993).

Penguin Books Ltd. for permission to reproduce 'Letter to Mr Wolf from H. Meeny' from *The Jolly Postman* by Janet and Allan Ahlberg (Viking, 1999), copyright © Allan and Janet Ahlberg 1986.

Vanessa Reilly for permission to reproduce an extract from her MA dissertation 'A Study of Teachers' Paralinguistic Behaviour in Classes for Young Learners of English to Inform a Local Action Research Project about Useful Strategies in the Young Learners' Classroom'.

Shelagh Rixon for permission to reproduce a photo of 'Boris the Second' published in *Tip Top 4* by Shelagh Rixon (Macmillan, 1993).

Scholastic UK Limited for 'Follow Up' taken from *Jet Primary Resource Book* 1996 (Mary Glasgow Magazines, 1996), copyright © Scholastic UK Limited t/a Mary Glasgow Magazines 1996.

Juliana Shak for an extract from 'Honest Omar and his cousin, Lucky Lucas, Day 3', reprinted by permission of the author.

The Society of Authors for the poem 'Mice' by Rose Fyleman, taken from *I like This Poem* (Penguin, 1979), copyright © The Estate of Rose Fyleman, reprinted by permission of The Society of Authors as the Literary Representative of the Estate of Rose Fyleman.

Walker Books Ltd. for permission to adapt 'The Grasshopper and the Ants' from *The Best Aesop's Fables* written by Margaret Clark and illustrated by Charlotte Voake (Walker Books Ltd, London, SE11 5HJ, 1990), text copyright © Margaret Clark 1990, reprinted by permission of the publisher.

Qiang Wang for permission to reproduce classroom observation data.

Although we have tried to trace and contact copyright holders before publication, in some cases this has not been possible. If contacted we will be pleased to rectify any errors or omissions at the earliest opportunity.

INTRODUCTION

Who is the book for and what kind of book is it?

This book is for experienced teachers with an interest in teaching English to children. It is for those teachers especially who wish to reflect on and explore their teaching in view of the discussion of the links between practice and theory. It is also intended for teacher trainers working with teachers on professional development courses. This book is not a resource manual that offers a list of ideas ready to be implemented in the classroom. Rather, it is a book that attempts to discuss and bring together research relevant to children and language learning and principles in classroom practice. Although it is my personal account, my hope is that individual teachers will engage with some ideas and questions discussed in this book and will develop them further in their own practice.

What age groups are covered in the term 'Young Learners'?

Primary education is very different in various parts of the world. In some contexts, primary school lasts from five to 11 years of age, while in other contexts children start school later, at the age of six or seven, and state primary school can carry on until children are 14 years of age, although primary school in these cases is often divided into lower and upper primary sections. Children may start learning English at different stages of their primary education or even before they are at school. In some contexts, children start learning English in kindergarten at the age of five or even earlier. In other contexts they may start at eight or ten. In order to embrace most contexts where English is taught to children, the ideas in this book can be applicable to all these age groups, from five to 14 years of age.

When discussing teaching principles and ideas for children, rigid age brackets such as four- to six-year-olds, seven- to nine-year-olds, ten- to

11-year-olds, or 12- to 14-year-olds would not work. Teachers and parents know that every child is unique and even in the same context there are often significant differences between children within the same age range. This is because children learn at their own speed; they change quickly and develop new skills and abilities in spurts. There are also substantial differences between, for example, eight-year-old children in different cultures and educational contexts. However, it would be equally problematic to leave the term 'Young Learners' entirely open as an umbrella term as it covers such a range of ages. In order to compromise and be more helpful to teachers, this book will tackle age groups on a continuum of younger to older learners, and offer in each chapter some principles and ideas for both ends of the continuum. The following table attempts to summarize features of the two ends of the continuum. This is a very basic starting point which will be elaborated on in later chapters.

Younger learners	Older learners
• Children are at pre-school or in the first couple of years of schooling.	• These children are well established at school and comfortable with school routines.
• Generally they have a holistic approach to language, which means that they understand meaningful messages but cannot analyse language yet.	• They show a growing interest in analytical approaches, which means that they begin to take an interest in language as an abstract system.
• They have lower levels of awareness about themselves as language learners as well as about process of learning.	• They show a growing level of awareness about themselves as language learners and their learning.
• They have limited reading and writing skills even in their first language.	• They have well developed skills as readers and writers.
• Generally, they are more concerned about themselves than others.	• They have a growing awareness of others and their viewpoints.
• They have a limited knowledge about the world.	• They have a growing awareness about the world around us.
• They enjoy fantasy, imagination, and movement.	• They begin to show interest in real life issues.

Characteristics of younger and older learners

These general descriptors for the two ends of the continuum can only serve as initial guidance for teachers. It is teachers' ultimate responsibility to place their own learners on the appropriate part of this continuum, based on their knowledge of their learners and their context. Teachers are in the best position to exercise their judgement about the suitability of the specific ideas suggested in the following chapters.

Variety of contexts

Teaching English to children has become a worldwide phenomenon due to the international expansion of English teaching combined with the general commitment of governments worldwide to reduce the starting age of learning English and include it in the curriculum in the primary school.

In some chapters an attempt has been made to embrace these differences, describing, for example, the variety of contexts where children may be learning English in different countries, at home or at school, in an English or a non-English environment. Many of the practical suggestions can be adapted to all kinds of contexts in either private or state schools in second and foreign language contexts. However, the main emphasis in the book remains on learning English as a foreign language.

Focus on teachers

In this book it is argued that teachers play a key role in the success of any teaching English to young learners (TEYL) programme. Their willingness and readiness to monitor the opportunities and limitations of their own contexts is the basis of success. It is also argued that teachers need time for reflection and experimentation so as to explore issues and questions in collaboration with children and other colleagues. Teachers may also want to foster positive and active relationships with parents, who are the most important sources of information about the children in their classes. It is to be hoped that this book will provide the inspiration for such explorations by offering a starting point with discussion of both the theory underlying practice and the principles that apply in the classroom.

What do the chapters offer?

The first chapter covers issues of general development and learning as a background to language learning, while the second chapter addresses first language learning so that teachers can familiarize themselves with where children are in their first language development. Building on this background, Chapter 3 moves on to issues of second language learning, covering a range of contexts where English is taught including English or non-English environments. This review aims to highlight the variations and circumstances that make a difference in learning and thus encourage teachers to begin to analyse carefully their own contexts. The next chapter discusses issues of policy and summarizes the factors of success of TEYL programmes. The hope is that armed with this information teachers can make the most of their circumstances but can also in some cases perhaps influence policy decisions in their own contexts. Following these background chapters, the second half of the book is devoted to the discussion of teaching the four language skills and the language system. Chapter 5 covers the teaching of listening and speaking, the two most important skills in TEYL programmes. Chapter 6 addresses issues of teaching reading and writing, highlighting the circumstances where it can be argued that the introduction of these two skills is beneficial. The next chapter discusses the teaching of the language system, both vocabulary and grammar in the same chapter. Chapter 8 turns to issues of 'learning to learn' underlining the importance of involving children in decisions concerning the learning process, linking with the discussion in previous parts of the book. The next chapter is devoted to coursebook evaluation and offers some basic principles of lesson planning and materials design. Chapter 10 deals with assessment, offering a variety of tools and useful principles for any context. Finally, the last chapter, Chapter 11, concludes the book with issues of researching TEYL classrooms: it covers aspects of research related to child subjects but it also offers some ideas to teachers who wish to initiate small-scale explorations into their own practice.

In addition, each chapter offers a list of recommended readings under two headings: (1) background theory and (2) practical teacher resources. Most chapters also contain examples of activities from a variety of internationally published children's coursebooks, resource books, and other teachers' materials to illustrate principles in practice. There is an appendix which offers tasks by means of which teachers can explore their own teaching, classroom materials, activities, and some classroom data. At the end of each chapter the reader will be recommended to look up particular tasks from the appendix which relate to the content of that chapter.

1 LEARNING AND DEVELOPMENT

Introduction

This first chapter is devoted to questions of how children develop and learn at home and at school. It will discuss how they learn new concepts and develop new ideas about the world, and how adults (parents, carers, and teachers) can help them make the process of learning as successful as possible. The aim is to make a link between what we know about children's development and learning in general and language learning in particular. It is important for language teachers to explore these links and take children's learning and their development in other areas into account. Many of the principles discussed in this chapter will be referred to and built on in subsequent chapters.

Active learning: 'constructivism'

Learning is an active process. All parents and teachers who have observed children in learning situations can testify just how actively they are involved when they are interested. For example, they can be completely absorbed in the story that they are listening to or in the pretend game that they are playing. When they are motivated, children are happy to try new things and to experiment with ideas and thoughts in conversations with adults and teachers. Children learn through their explorations and play, and through opportunities to talk things through with others, usually adults. Exploring can refer to things in concrete terms (for example, playing with sand and water or building with toy bricks) or in abstract terms in conversations with others. Often the two happen simultaneously, for example, children and adults can play together with water and sand and talk about what they are doing.

Jean Piaget (1896–1980), who began to develop his ideas in the first half of the twentieth century, was one of the most famous child psychologists of all times. He referred to active learning as 'constructivism'. He suggested that children construct knowledge for themselves by actively making sense of their environment. For example, a young child might know that baby birds such as chicks and ducklings are hatched from eggs. When this child comes across other animals during a visit to a farm, he or she assumes that the pigs are hatched from eggs, too. According to Piaget, this is the process of 'assimilation'. The child is assimilating information to fit his or her own interpretation of the world and existing ways of thinking (i.e. all animals are hatched from eggs). At a later stage, maybe, in a conversation about animals, a parent might explain that piglets are not hatched from eggs. At this point the child will have to adapt or change his or her way of thinking to accommodate this new idea. Piaget refers to this process as 'accommodation'. Without this adaptation—something that the child has to do for himself— learning would not take place. Assimilation and accommodation thus describe two sides of the same process, i.e. learning. Such interaction between the environment and children's existing knowledge is ongoing and throughout the years further and further refinements are added to the growing knowledge base. In this way, children are active constructors of their knowledge of the world.

Piaget's stages of development

Teachers and parents can often judge very well what their children can or cannot yet do or understand. Even though children are all unique learners, they also show some characteristics in common with their peers. When parents of similar-aged children talk together they often realize that their children act similarly in a range of situations. For example, parents of five-year-olds find that their children use similar arguments in conversations or enjoy very similar games, activities, and jokes.

Such similarities within age bands were observed by Piaget too, and he developed his famous framework which suggests that there are four universal stages of development that all children go through. Piaget and his colleagues constructed tasks and conducted experiments based on this theory and produced a detailed description of the four stages. In 1923 Piaget published a book called *The Language and the Thought of the Child* in which he argued that development was a process of acquiring the principles of formal logic. He referred to basic logical abilities as 'operations', hence the naming of the stages. Each child follows these stages in exactly the same order, and development unfolds as a result of the biological processes of growth, and the development of the child's brain. Table 1.1 summarizes the main characteristics of children's development within each 'Piagetian' stage.

It is useful for teachers to be familiar with the Piagetian framework because teaching English to children can mean working with very different age groups with different interests and needs. Teaching a class of 12-year-olds

Sensori-motor stage (from birth to two years of age)
- The young child learns to interact with the environment by manipulating objects around him.

Pre-operational stage (from two to seven years of age)
- The child's thinking is largely reliant on perception but he or she gradually becomes more and more capable of logical thinking. On the whole this stage is characterized by egocentrism (a kind of self-centredness) and a lack of logical thinking.

Concrete operational stage (from seven to eleven years of age)
- Year 7 is the 'turning point' in cognitive development because children's thinking begins to resemble 'logical' adult-like thinking. They develop the ability to apply logical reasoning in several areas of knowledge at the same time (such as maths, science, or map reading) but this ability is restricted to the immediate context. This means that children at this stage cannot yet generalize their understanding.

Formal operational stage (from eleven years onwards)
- Children are able to think beyond the immediate context in more abstract terms. They are able to carry out logical operations such as deductive reasoning in a systematic way. They achieve 'formal logic'.

Table 1.1: Piagetian stages of development

requires very different materials, methods, and teaching style from a class of six-year-olds. Given that the starting age for language learning seems to be going down in most contexts (see Chapter 4 on policy), the majority of teachers will probably have to be able to respond to the needs and interest of various age groups, including those in the Piagetian pre-operational stage.

Piaget's 'thinking' revolution: from pre-operational to operational stage

It is worth exploring Piaget's 'thinking revolution' in a bit more detail. Piaget's assessment of children under seven years of age was that they were lacking logical thinking. Instead, young children are characterized by 'egocentrism', which means that they typically look at the world around them from their own point of view and they find it difficult, if not impossible, to appreciate someone else's point of view. One of Piaget's famous experiments was the so-called 'Three mountain experiment' (see Figure 1.1). In this exercise Piaget and his colleagues asked young children to walk around a three-dimensional display of three mountains where each mountain was distinguished by a different colour and a distinctive summit. Once the children had had a chance to look at the mountains, the experimenters placed a doll at the opposite side of the display facing the children from the other end. At this point they asked the children to choose a photo which showed the doll's perspective. Typically, children under the age of seven in this experiment were unable to choose the correct photo. Instead, they chose the photo which was identical to their own perspective. This was considered as proof of these children's egocentrism.

Figure 1.1: The three mountain experiment

Many tasks similar to the one above were given to children of seven years of age and younger. Some of these tasks tested 'conservation', i.e. the understanding that moving two sticks of the same length away from each other does not change their length, or that pouring water from one container into another does not add or take away anything from the original amount of water. Other tasks tested 'class inclusion', i.e. the relationship of subcategories and main categories and principles of hierarchy, for example, how the concepts of animals, types of animals like dogs, and types of dogs like terriers relate to each other. Typically, the great majority of children under the age of seven gave incorrect answers to all the questions. Piaget concluded that their development had not reached the stage where they could have applied the rules of logic.

Criticism of Piaget's stages

The pre-operational stage

Both parents and teachers worldwide may feel that Piaget's assessment of children under the age of seven was a bit harsh. One of Piaget's main critics was Margaret Donaldson, the Scottish child psychologist. She suggested that Piaget underestimated young children. First of all, the language used by Piaget and his colleagues in the tasks was confusing for them. In particular, the questions Piaget and his colleagues asked were unnatural and ambiguous. For example, 'Are there more yellow flowers or flowers in this picture?' was a typical question that was put to the children in one of the class inclusion tasks. Donaldson argued that questions like this were uncommon in everyday language use and that the children could not make sense of them. Another source of criticism was the context of the Piagetian experiments. Many children failed because they misunderstood the context. For example, in the conservation tasks when the adult experimenter rearranged the sticks, the children expected a change as a result of the adult's manipulation of the objects. Many children thought that something must have changed, otherwise it would not make sense to ask the same question again. Donaldson decided to redesign some of the original experiments in a more child-friendly format. In a book published in 1978 entitled *Children's Minds*, Margaret Donaldson reported that once these tasks were presented in a familiar context, the majority of the results for children under the age of seven improved. In fact, it has repeatedly been demonstrated that when young children are presented with familiar tasks, in familiar circumstances, introduced by familiar adults using language that makes sense to them, they show signs of logical thinking much earlier than Piaget claimed. These findings and criticisms have important implications for teachers, in particular with regard to issues of testing and assessment in young learners' classrooms. Unfamiliar tasks, unfamiliar contexts, and unfamiliar adults can cause children anxiety and as a result they may perform well below their true ability or not respond at all to the questions or tasks.

The operational stages

Even though the most important criticisms concerned Piaget's preoperational stage, the description of operational stages turned out to be problematic, too. Children between the ages of seven and 11 all develop formal thinking to some extent but this is usually due to their schooling which promotes such thinking. However, their contexts and cultural practices vary greatly and this leads to a great deal of variety across this age group worldwide. With regard to the final stage, Piaget's descriptions were simply overconfident. The ultimate intellectual challenge of being able to think according to the rules of formal logic is not actually fully and automatically achieved by all teenagers or even adults. Indeed, people do not need to think in a logical fashion in most everyday contexts. Analytical development leading to formal logic is also the result of formal schooling rather than natural maturation and different educational systems contribute to maintaining differences between same-aged children or teenagers in different parts of the world. In addition, it is also reasonable to propose that development does not actually stop at the age of eleven or twelve but continues well beyond this age, well beyond Piaget's last stage.

While it is true that Piaget's original ideas have been challenged, most developmental psychologists would still support the existence of some stage-like development in children even though the stages are believed to be less rigid and perhaps less deterministic than originally suggested by Piaget. What is important for teachers to learn from Piaget's theory? It is important for teachers to be sensitive and open to the needs and interests of various age groups and continually monitor their changing needs. Careful monitoring and regular feedback from children will help teachers select suitable materials that are developmentally appropriate for the given age group in a given context. As stated in the Introduction of this book, particular attention will be paid to differentiating between the needs of younger and older children. In the following chapters, where appropriate, principles underlying the use of tasks, activities, and other materials with both younger and older children will be offered.

The role of interaction: 'social constructivism'

Vygotsky's theory of learning

With the stage theory, Piaget emphasized the biological basis of development and the universal progression from stage to stage in every child. However, there is an important social side to children's development too. The social environment, the cultural context, and in particular the influence of peers, teachers, and parents engaged in interactions with children are also major sources of learning and development.

Social constructivism is associated with the ideas of the Russian psychologist, Lev Vygotsky (1896–1934). Vygotsky was a contemporary of Piaget and shared some of his basic beliefs about child development. He agreed with Piaget that children construct knowledge for themselves and that they actively participate in the learning process. However, he pointed out that the social environment too has an important role to play. In his book entitled *Mind and Society, the Development of Higher Mental Processes* (translated into English in 1978), he explored the role of culture and social context. He turned teachers' and parents' attention to the powerful effect of the social context: hence 'social' is added to constructivism. Quite apart from which Piagetian stage a child belonged to, Vygotsky was interested in the learning potential of the individual, recognizing the fact that all children were unique learners. He was interested to explore what individual children were capable of achieving with the help and support of a more knowledgeable partner.

Accordingly, the most famous Vygotskian concept was born, the 'Zone of Proximal Development' (or, as it is often referred to, the 'ZPD'). This concept describes the difference or the 'zone' between the current knowledge of the child and the potential knowledge achievable with some help from a more knowledgeable peer or adult. Vygotsky argues that working within the ZPD is a fertile ground for learning because it starts with what the child already knows and carefully builds on it according to the child's immediate needs to go forward. Figure 1.2 gives a visual representation of the ZPD.

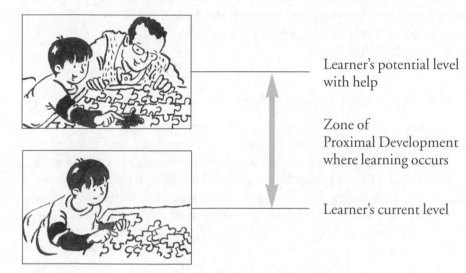

Learner's potential level with help

Zone of
Proximal Development
where learning occurs

Learner's current level

Figure 1.2: The Zone of of Proximal Development

For example, think of a four-year-old boy who is sitting down to share a story book with a parent when he notices that the cover page of the story book is full of colourful stars. He is eager to start counting the stars and he is able to count up to about 15 or 16 but beyond that he gets confused with the counting. He will say things like 'twenty ten' instead of thirty, leave out some numbers altogether, or just stop, not knowing how to carry on. Left to his own devices, he will probably abandon the task of counting. However, a parent or teacher, or even an older brother or sister, can help him to continue. They can prompt him by inserting the next correct number or by giving a visual clue (for example, showing the number of fingers) or by pronouncing the first sound of the word (*twenty-fff*) that follows.

Helping children to learn by offering systematic support

Given this kind of help, the child may be able to count up to 50 or even 100. When such help is provided in a systematic manner, it is often referred to as 'scaffolding'. Building on both Piaget's and Vygotsky's theory and work, Jerome Bruner, an American psychologist, and his colleagues, introduced this term in 1976 (see also Wood, Bruner, and Ross). Scaffolding is essentially an instructional strategy which ensures that the child can gain confidence and take control of the task (for example, counting the stars) or parts of the task as soon as he or she is willing and able to. At the same time, he or she is offered immediate, meaningful support whenever stuck. During the interaction that takes place in the ZPD, the adult encourages the child with praise, points out possible difficulties, and makes sure distractions are avoided. The adult also ensures that the learner stays on track and is motivated to finish the task. The support is carefully adjusted to the needs of the individual child.

The importance of language for learning

The language used in interactions with parents and teachers is important because it is the vehicle through which understanding and learning take place. It is language that allows us to make messages accessible to our listeners. It is language that allows us to ask questions and clarify what is not clear, and it is language that allows us to express our ideas with great precision. According to Vygotsky, all learning happens in social interactions with others. Learning occurs in conversations, as a result of understanding and interpreting for ourselves what others are saying. At the beginning, when children are very young, parents support them by explaining new ideas carefully, by repeating information in different contexts until they are satisfied that the messages have got through. In other words, early on, adults take responsibility for, or 'regulate', children's learning. One of the most important tools parents use to regulate their children's learning is language, in particular, dialogues. Using language, they remind children what they already know, explain how to go about solving problems, and in general support their learning. Later on, children learn to signal when something is not clear or ask questions to clarify a point. As children mature, they learn to regulate more and more aspects of their learning. Chapter 2 will discuss the crucial role of carers' language to children in more detail and Chapter 8 will explore children's development in taking more responsibility for their learning.

The significance of language has important implications for teacher talk in all classrooms, including of course the foreign or second language classroom. For example, EYL teachers need to be aware that their language use is often the main source of language input. Children learn new language forms in meaningful contexts so listening to the teacher is essential both for modelling pronunciation and for providing opportunities for understanding new input from context. Children also need opportunities to join in and interact with the teacher and with each other. Teachers will need to think about how they can best scaffold children's early language production in their English classes, what questioning techniques they will use to elicit language from their learners, and how they can encourage children to use language meaningfully with each other.

Children are all unique learners

Gardner's framework for multiple intelligences

Having considered how similarly-aged children share certain characteristics (Piaget) and how the social environment, in particular social interaction with parents and teachers, can make a difference in terms of offering unique, enriching experiences (Vygotsky), I shall now explore the issue of uniqueness.

Teachers and parents often notice that individual children enjoy different activities. For example, if we take working with stories, children who are musical often enjoy singing and dancing and expressing themselves through drama and ballet. At the same time, they may show very little interest in writing, drawing, or colouring. Other children might get embarrassed if asked to join in with singing and dancing but enjoy writing or drawing based on the story. When assessing children's intelligence, many psychologists have argued for the need to take such differences in individuals into account. Howard Gardner, an American psychologist, in a publication entitled *Frames of Mind: Theory of Multiple Intelligences* (1983) suggested that intelligence had no unitary character, rather, it manifested itself in many different ways in different children. He refers to these multiple intelligences as 'frames of mind'. The types of intelligences are linguistic, logico-mathematical, musical, spatial, bodily/kinaesthetic, interpersonal, intra-personal, and natural. New ideas and new practical interpretations with regard to the types of basic intelligences are constantly developing and Table 1.2 merely summarizes the main features of each type of intelligence.

According to Gardner's framework, in the example about working with stories, the first group of children would be described as showing particular strengths in the areas of musical and bodily/kinaesthetic intelligences while the second group exhibit linguistic and spatial intelligences. Teachers who are aware of this framework can ensure that their teaching is meaningful to all children with any one or any combination of these intelligences.

Learning styles

These descriptions of intelligences can be related to another term commonly used in the educational literature, i.e. 'learning styles'. Styles can describe personality types such as more careful and reflective children as opposed to

Linguistic:	sensitivity to the sound, rhythm, and meaning of words and the different functions of language
Logico-mathematical:	sensitivity to and capacity to detect logical and numerical patterns, ability to handle long chains of logical reasoning
Musical:	ability to produce or appreciate pitch, rhythm, or melody and aesthetic-sounding tones, understanding of the forms of musical expressiveness
Spatial:	ability to perceive the visual/spatial world accurately, to perform transformations on those perceptions, and to recreate aspects of visual experience in the absence of relevant stimuli
Bodily-kinaesthetic:	ability to use the body skilfully for expressive as well as goal oriented purposes, ability to handle objects skilfully
Interpersonal:	ability to detect and respond appropriately to the moods, temperaments, motivations, and intentions of others
Intrapersonal:	ability to discriminate complex inner feelings and to use them to guide one's own behaviour, knowledge of one's own strengths, weaknesses, desires, and intelligences
Naturalist:	ability to recognize and classify varieties of animals, minerals, and plants

Table 1.2: Gardner's Multiple Intelligences. Adapted from L. Berk: Child Development, *Allyn and Bacon 2005.*

impulsive and more interactive children. Other styles, related to personality features, describe cognitive categories such as analytic or global learners. Analytic learners are those with an attention to detail and global learners are those who are more holistic in their approach. Finally, some styles describe perceptual differences. Some children prefer listening to new input while others need lots of visual stimulus. Yet others are kinaesthetic, which means that they like to feel and touch things and move their body in expressive ways to aid their learning and communication.

It is important for teachers to take into account that all children have stronger and weaker aspects of their multiple intelligences and preferred learning styles. Some of the early preferences and styles might change with time but there will always be a variety of learners in every class. Therefore teachers need to incorporate a variety of activities into second and foreign language classrooms to ensure that everybody's preferences are catered for at least some of the time. For example, when new rhymes or songs are introduced in an English class, it is a good idea to present them using a variety of techniques. Children can listen to the teacher or the tape saying or singing the rhyme or the song. This will cater for learners with an auditory preference. Children can also look at the text of the song or the rhyme in the book or look at the illustrations. This activity will cater for visual learners. Finally, children can watch the teacher miming the actions and join in with the words and actions, too. This will cater for kinaesthetic learners. Incorporating various 'senses' also makes learning memorable and fun. Once aware of having to cater for different intelligences, teachers can make their lessons more accessible to all children.

Exceptional children and mixed ability classes

In almost all contexts teachers will have to deal with exceptional children: children with very high ability or slower learners with emotional and/or learning difficulties of various types. Many teachers work with large mixed ability classes and they face a similar sort of problem when they have to cater for different needs within the same class. It is essential that all children of all abilities find learning a new language a motivating and rewarding exercise and that they can progress at their own pace. It is the teacher's challenge to provide them with suitable tasks and rewards according to their individual needs. Exceptionally gifted children will need to learn early on to work independently so that they can carry on with motivating tasks while the rest of the class are engaged in something else. Similarly, slower learners need suitably challenging tasks and special support that will keep them motivated and ensure small successes. Children of all abilities will enjoy working together in pairs or small groups and more capable learners can often help weaker ones. These considerations might lead to dividing children into ability groups some of the time and helping them to learn to work independently at other times. It is important for teachers to monitor children's progress carefully because they can develop new strengths and interests over time and they go through spurts of development and other 'ups and downs'. For example, young children are often affected by events at home such as the birth of a brother or sister, a lost teddy, or a parent being away from home, and their performance at school might decline temporarily. It is a good idea for teachers to keep in touch with parents and work together to solve problems.

Summary

Children within the same age groups may show similar characteristics but at the same time they are also very different as individuals with their strengths and preferences as learners. While teachers can benefit from familiarizing themselves with the universal aspects of children's development, it is also important that this is balanced out with focus on the individual child. Teachers will have to use their best judgement in deciding about the most suitable materials and techniques to fit their learners of different ages in different contexts. Learning about the children by talking to them, observing them, and talking to their parents can help teachers to understand the children they are working with. By incorporating variety into everyday practice, teachers of children can make their lessons full of stimulation for all learner types and intelligences.

Recommended reading

Background theory

Berk, L. 2005. *Child Development.* Boston: Allyn and Bacon.

This is a comprehensive book on child psychology which covers cognitive, emotional, and social development from birth to adolescence. It is of interest to those teachers who want to refresh their knowledge about child development in general.

Cohen, D. 2002. *How the Child's Mind Develops.* Hove: Routledge.

This is a thought-provoking and entertaining account of child development for both interested parents and teachers. The main theories are summarized in a highly accessible manner. The book contains many interesting topics such as the effect of television and computers on children.

Donaldson, M. 1978. *Children's Minds.* London: Fontana Press.

This book explores the effect of school on children's development. It describes the demands of a new mode of thinking required by school and the nature of difficulties children face but it also offers suggestions to parents and teachers with regard to how they can help children to cope with these difficulties.

Grieve, R. and **M. Hughes** (eds.). 1990. *Understanding Children.* Oxford: Oxford University Press.

This book covers areas including language development, reading, writing, picture drawing, and perceptions in separate essays written by established researchers in each field.

Wood, D. 1998. *How Children Think and Learn.* Oxford: Blackwell Publishers.

This book covers language development and cognitive development. Wood reviews theoretical debates in psychology and offers a synthesis of what is known about children's thinking and learning.

Tasks

If you would like to look at some practical tasks to explore your own practice related to the content of this chapter, you can try Tasks 1: 'Exploring different age groups' and 2: 'Observing teachers' language use' (Appendix pages 155 and 157).

2 LEARNING THE FIRST LANGUAGE AT HOME AND AT SCHOOL

Introduction

In the first chapter, development in childhood in very general terms was considered and although some examples have already been introduced to show the relevance of these ideas to language learning, language learning has not yet been explored in detail.

In this chapter the focus will be on learning the first language as there may be parallels in the processes of children learning the first, the second, and the third languages. Looking at first language learning can offer important insights to teachers about the rate and nature of development and the continuity between learning the first language and other languages.

Why is first language development of interest to EYL teachers?

The comparison between first and second language learning is relevant and important because children in second or foreign language classes are still in the process of learning their mother tongue. First language acquisition is a long process that continues well beyond childhood, so by definition, it cannot be complete for any child learner. Depending on the starting age, these two processes can be more or less closely intertwined. The younger the child is, the more similar the two processes will be, because very young children lack the ability to manipulate and think about language in a conscious way. This is especially true for children in immersion environments.

How are child learners different from adults?

Adult learners can rely on a number of useful resources when they learn a new language. They can analyse language in an abstract way. This ability will allow them to compare patterns and linguistic forms that are similar or different in their mother tongue and in the other language. Knowing at least one language very well, adult learners can hypothesize quite deliberately about features of another language. For example, an English native speaker may hypothesize that past tense verb forms in German (a closely related language) can be either regular or irregular, just as in English. Such a conscious attitude might lead the adult learner to notice verb features in German earlier. Adults can use their knowledge of the world and different contexts to make guesses about unknown words or phrases. They also have a good understanding of the rules of communication. For example, for something as simple and straightforward as everyday conversation, they know that they have to use set phrases to open and close the conversation and they need to judge the level of politeness depending on who they are talking to. Mature language learners also use a variety of strategies that help them to memorize and rehearse patterns and words and they regularly reflect on how well they are doing.

By contrast, children cannot make use of these advantages yet, or at least there are significant differences between various age groups in the extent to which they can do so. For example, a class of six-year-olds will be largely unable to reflect on how their first language works, and will show no interest or inclination to notice language forms in either their first or second language. They will pick up and learn the second or foreign language if they are having fun and if they can work out messages from meaningful contexts. This means learning holistically without attention to abstract language forms. As we progress to older children, their first language development will allow them more and more opportunities for useful comparisons between the languages they know. Their growing abilities in their mother tongue, for example, to construct phrases, sentences, or questions, create and retell stories, or to hold a conversation, will all be important direct or indirect sources of support in the process of learning another language.

Universal processes in language learning

Another reason why it is important to consider first language development is that research shows that there are many universal aspects of language development whatever language (first or second language) and whatever type of learner (adult or child) we consider. For example, in both first language and second language learning in English there is a stage of development where speakers omit auxiliaries (for example, 'do' or 'does') such as in the sentence '*Where you going?' or the third person singular marker 's', such as in the sentence '*He like singing' (an asterisk * denotes an incorrect form). There is also a universal order of acquisition with regard to many aspects of English morphology (word structure). For example, in verb forms, morphemes include '-*ing*' ending or '-*s*' for third person singular. Particularly striking is the similarity between the order of acquisition by

English mother tongue learners and naturalistic English as a second language learners, i.e. those who learn the language immersed in an English environment. In the case of children who are learning a second language in regular timetabled classrooms, the relative lack of input and the type of instruction can of course alter this order. However, the natural order is still relevant for teachers. For example, many teachers I have worked with mentioned that they noticed mistakes in their learners' speech and writing to do with the third person -*s* even though this grammatical feature is often covered right at the beginning of children's courses. For example, in the sentence 'She sleeps late on Sundays', they omit the -*s* in the verb. The fact that learners later in the course still make this mistake indicates that the third person -*s* may be naturally acquired much later than originally thought. Spending too much time and effort in the classroom to eradicate it may well be a fruitless exercise.

How is the first language acquired?

The role of input and interaction

Provided that the necessary input and opportunities for interaction are available, all children learn their mother tongue fairly effortlessly and can communicate in familiar contexts by the time they are four or five years old. All babies and young children need to be talked to so that they can receive input and begin to learn to participate in interactions. All humans have the inborn capacity to produce baby talk, special simplified talk directed to babies. Even children do this with their younger siblings. Research in the 1970s, such as the study by Catherine Snow in 1972, showed that mothers' speech to their babies was slower and more repetitive than their normal speech to adults. They used various simplifications and modifications in their speech and these were shown to be very helpful in making the input comprehensible to children. Such simplified talk contains a lot of repetition, a slower rate of speech, exaggerated intonation patterns, and the use of higher pitch. With regard to content, carers typically talk about topic areas immediately relevant to the child such as the family, home environment, toys, animals, body parts, and food.

The role of Universal Grammar

Whilst children are learning from input and interactions with their parents, their inborn capacities are also at work. Noam Chomsky, one of the best known linguists of the twentieth century, argued that children often produced language that they could not have heard in natural interaction with others. For example, all children learning English as their mother tongue produce past tense constructions such as *flyed, *writed, and *buyed.

They are attaching the regular past tense marker to irregular verbs. Chomsky argues that these constructions show evidence that children make constant efforts to hypothesize about the structure of the language. Based on these, Chomsky proposed the theory of Universal Grammar (UG), which can be imagined as a kind of a device containing representations of abstract facts about human language. He proposed that all humans are born with the capacity to build on UG. Exposure to input in the given language sets the various parameters of the UG and this enables children to learn particular languages. For example, when a baby is born into an English-speaking environment, his or her UG helps the baby to recognize that English is a language where the word order is typically SVO (subject, verb, and object) rather than VSO, as for example, for Irish. As a result, the baby can start producing early utterances such as 'Daddy sleep' rather than 'Sleep daddy'.

The achievements of the first five years

Language development starts well before children are able to say anything. In the beginning, babies exercise their receptive skills, and only with considerable delay do they start producing language. It takes several years to move slowly from fragmented language use to a fully productive command of the language. In English, children progress from one-word utterances (such as mummy, daddy) to two-word (mummy go) and three word (where mummy gone) utterances. Different children have so called 'language bursts' at different times but typically during the second year of their lives they acquire a huge amount of vocabulary and begin to tackle the grammar of English. Word learning takes place at an astonishing speed. A great deal of guesswork goes on in both listening and speaking, for example, words are often used before they are understood fully. The developments in understanding and production are interrelated and gradual. Learning English grammar requires tackling patterns that often have a multifunctional purpose. This means that the same form is used for different functions. For example, 'get' is used in different ways, such as 'get up', 'get someone an ice cream', and 'get someone to go to sleep'. Children will acquire an item for a single purpose first and gradually add other functions.

During these early years, children are immensely creative with language and enjoy playing with words. They make up their own words, create jokes, and experiment with language even when they have to rely on limited resources. The following examples come from children I have worked with. One child called a cactus a 'hedgehog flower' because he had learnt the word 'hedgehog' and was looking for a way to name a plant that looked like a hedgehog. Another child who had chicken pox and was covered in spots saw a Dalmatian and referred to it as 'a dog with chicken pox' because the spots on the dog reminded him of his own spots. The implication here for teachers is that, given appropriate opportunities, creativity and willingness to play with the language could carry over to the learning of second and foreign languages as well. Teachers can encourage children to experiment with language and enjoy language for its own sake. Drama activities or simple poetry writing, for example, which allow children's imagination and fantasy to flourish, can be regular activities in EYL classrooms. Language play can take many other forms such as playing with forms, sounds, rhyme, rhythm, creating imaginary words or nonsense words.

By the time they are four or five, most children have acquired their first language more or less fully in terms of the basic grammatical control and lexis needed for normal conversations. However, whilst five-year-olds are effective communicators in the home environment, they still have a long way to go in terms of continuing to learn their mother tongue for communicating with people outside that environment, in particular in more formal contexts and unfamiliar settings.

Whilst it is true that the processes of first language acquisition in early childhood (before age five in one's mother tongue) are quite different from learning a new language in primary school contexts, this review of early development is interesting to teachers of English as a second or foreign language for a number of reasons. For example, it is important for teachers to appreciate just how long it takes for children to learn even their mother tongue. In some contexts, children as young as five years old (and sometimes even younger) start a new language. Having some awareness about what a five-year-old child can say and do in his or her first language can help teachers to appreciate what is realistic for that age group in a second language. It is generally a good idea to monitor children's abilities in their mother tongue in order to inform second or foreign language teaching and learning.

This brief review is based on learning English rather any other languages. Although many principles may hold true for other languages as well, teachers of English to children of various mother tongues will always find it useful to understand more about the children's first language development, whatever that language may be.

The influence of school on first language development

Language use at home

At home with parents and siblings, children are already confident communicators. Their parents share most of their experiences, which makes it easier to talk about things. Parents also tend to take the lead in conversations and are eager to work out their children's half-formed ideas. There is no need to be explicit and precise with language use at home. Parents naturally scaffold their children's language in dialogues as discussed in Chapter 1. Whilst at home most communication is embedded in the shared immediate context, school language use is more independent of immediate contexts. Teachers do not know children as well as parents and their understanding of the children's experiences is limited, which makes it harder to work out what children mean. It is often difficult for young children to make the jump from home to school language use, i.e. from implicit to more explicit ways of using their first language. Studies show that rich linguistic interactions between parents or carers and their children at home can be important in preparing children to be successful communicators at school. Gordon Wells and his colleagues conducted studies (1981 and 1985) which showed that 'good' interactions offer corrections, valuable feedback, and supportive encouragement. Children who are talked to and read to on a regular basis, and who have the chance to initiate ideas for joint exploration in dialogues with parents, start with a great advantage at school.

Language use at school

At school children are often required to talk about past experiences, future plans, or other people's perspectives, i.e. things that are not related to the immediate context. At school children will continue learning about their first language. They may come across a standard version of their first language which might be quite different from a dialect used at home. With regard to more complex grammar, they will learn to handle clause types, complex sentences, and the rules of connecting ideas in speaking as well as writing. They will also acquire formal, literary, historic, and archaic phrases and come in contact with varieties of their mother tongue, such as other regional accents. Throughout the school years, the rate of vocabulary learning will continue to be very high. Susan Foster-Cohen (1999), a researcher interested in first language development, reports that an average eight- or nine-year-old knows between 4,000 and 10,000 words and it is estimated that about 800 to 1,200 words are learnt at school every year from this age onwards. This is a staggering amount of new vocabulary to learn. Children will also learn about various spoken and written genres such as stories, plays, letters, descriptions, or science reports. The process of becoming confident readers and writers in their first language will continue into the years of secondary schooling.

Organizing school knowledge and experiences

Monitoring own learning

In addition to learning subject content such as geography, history, maths, science, or English at school, children also need to learn to begin to monitor their own learning. This is often referred to as children's growing metacognitive ability. Development in their ability to plan, monitor, and evaluate their performance and their learning will increase as children progress through the school years. These ideas will be explored further in Chapter 8, on 'learning to learn'. In both first and second languages they will gradually learn to stand back from and think about language in an abstract way, and reflect on what they can do or would like to be able to do. For example, during primary school children learn to define words, appreciate multiple meanings or puns, riddles, and metaphors in their mother tongue. All these learning experiences require that they analyse language as an abstract system. The emerging ability to think about language as a system has important implications for second and foreign language learning and opens up possibilities of analysing, comparing, and discussing language forms in the second or foreign language classroom.

Memory development

The ability to remember facts, figures, and labels, such as the capital city of France, sums in mathematics, names of famous people and important dates, or words in a foreign language are tasks that require effective memory strategies. These strategies also generally improve with age. Research shows that expertise has an important influence on children's memory performance. Children who know a particular area or topic well show increasingly superior memory capacities for retrieval as compared to those who do not. Two out of many interesting studies that report on findings in this area were carried out by Michelene Chi in 1978 and Wolfgang Schneider and David Bjorklund in 1992. Both of these studies looked at the ability of children to recall items with and without some background knowledge of the topic.

Chi gave pictures of chessboard arrangements to expert child chess players and adults who knew how to play chess but were not experts. Chi found that the expert children recalled the chessboard combinations much better than the adults because of their knowledge of chess and their ability to remember chess patterns rather than individual items. Wolfgang Schneider and David Bjorklund gave a list of soccer related words to learn and remember to a group of children who were experts in soccer and to another group who were not experts. The findings showed that the experts remembered far more items from the soccer list than the non-experts did. The implication of these findings for teachers of English as a second language to children is that it is important to find out what their children are good at and what they know about. Whether it is dinosaurs, butterflies, spaceships, or sports that the children are interested in, remembering and retrieving new vocabulary will be a lot easier for them if they know about the topic and are enthusiastic about it.

Summary

There are important parallels between children's first language and second language development and TEYL teachers can benefit from being familiar with first language processes. It is important to know what children can do and like doing in their mother tongue because teachers can usefully build on this knowledge in their second or foreign language classes.

Recommended reading

Background theory

Foster-Cohen, S. H. 1999. *An Introduction to Child Language Development.* London: Longman.

This is an accessible theoretical account of first language development in childhood. The theory is balanced with tasks and interesting data to reflect on.

Corden, R. 2000. *Literacy and Learning through Talk: Strategies for the Primary Classroom.* Buckingham: Open University Press.

This book is focused on literacy teaching in English-speaking primary classrooms and it explores the features of effective interpersonal communication. Teachers can find advice about setting up speaking activities in class.

Cook, G. 2000. *Language Play, Language Learning.* Oxford: Oxford University Press.

This book explores the implications of language play for language teaching and emphasizes the role of ritual. It is argued that language play is an important aspect of language learning which needs more attention in classrooms.

Lightbown, P. M. and N. Spada. 2006. *How Languages are Learned.* (3rd edition). Oxford: Oxford University Press.

This is a classic book for both language teachers and students specializing in language studies. It is a highly accessible account of theories of both first and second language learning. The book contains practical activities and questionnaires to bring the theory alive.

Lloyd, P. 1997. 'Children's communication' in Grieve, R. and Hughes, M. (eds.): *Understanding Children.* Oxford: Blackwell.

This chapter explores children's growing ability to handle communication tasks which require explicit referencing and paying attention to each other's messages.

Tasks

If you would like to look at some practical tasks to explore your own practice related to the content of this chapter, you can try Task 3: Exploring children's first language performances (Appendix page 158).

3 LEARNING A SECOND/ THIRD LANGUAGE AT HOME AND AT SCHOOL

Introduction

There is an enormous variety in the world with regard to at what age, how, and why children learn other languages. This chapter will outline some of these circumstances, starting with natural acquisition of two languages at birth, moving on to beginning to learn new languages a bit later but while still quite young. Important differences between the demands of learning a language in informal situations such as everyday conversations and more formal learning such as at school will be discussed. This brief overview of second language contexts will compare ESL (English as a second language) contexts where English is taught in an English environment and EFL (English as a foreign language) contexts where English is taught as a time-tabled subject in a non-English environment. These comparisons are useful to teachers because they can develop realistic expectations with regard to both themselves and their learners, their achievements, opportunities, and limitations in their own contexts.

Early bilingualism

The earliest possible chance to learn two languages is to start at birth. This early process is often referred to as the 'simultaneous acquisition' of two or sometimes more languages. In a mixed nationality marriage, for example, one parent may use French only with the children while the other parent uses English only. Suzanne Romaine, a well known researcher in the area of bilingual studies, refers to this as the 'one person one language' scenario (1995). When this strategy is systematically followed by both parents, children can acquire two languages at the same time. Differences between the levels of competence in the two languages will of course always be inevitable due to factors such as which language is dominant in the society and whether or not the parents speak or understand each other's languages.

Bilingual children, compared to their monolingual peers, generally appear to develop more slowly in linguistic terms. For example, referring back to the developments of the first five years in Chapter 2, bilingual children may say their first words a little later and learn fewer words and grammatical structures. However, this is not strictly true of all bilinguals. Some children, who have more extroverted personalities and like taking risks, might start talking just as early as monolinguals.

Bilingual children go through a phase of mixing the languages in the first two years. Then, at around three years of age they start to separate the two languages and will begin to address people in different languages depending on their relevant language background. Some researchers consider this the truly bilingual stage. However, when and to what extent this happens also depends on social factors such as the extent to which parents attract the child's attention to the existence of two languages and the attitude children acquire to the two languages. Even in the case of early bilinguals, the development of both languages will continue in a balanced way only if opportunities are regularly available to practise and develop competence in both languages. Schooling will be a major source of further development. Almost all bilingual children will grow up to function in their dominant language, which is the medium of instruction at school.

For a long time it was believed that learning two languages at the same time was detrimental to children's development. However, research in the last 30 years, especially in Canada, has now convincingly demonstrated that this is not the case. Merrill Swain and her colleagues in Canada have shown that in fact quite the opposite is true (see Swain 2000b). Bilingualism is advantageous for children, especially with regard to their early metalinguistic awareness, i.e. their ability to manipulate and label language. As they are exposed to two languages, bilingual children are more aware of language systems. For example, they realize earlier than monolinguals that words are arbitrary symbols and the same object can be referred to by using different labels. In general they are more conscious of language structures and patterns and learn to reflect on these earlier.

The effect of age

Critical Period Hypothesis

Turning to those children who do not start two languages at birth, what are the benefits of learning languages young, i.e. still in childhood? Folk wisdom holds that children are very successful language learners. It has been observed repeatedly that children who move to another country pick up the new language seemingly effortlessly and quickly as opposed to their parents who often find language learning more of a challenge. This observation led to assumptions about the advantages of starting learning a second language young and also to a great deal of enthusiasm around the world for intro-ducing English in primary school or even earlier. One reason why early language learning has become so popular is that many psycholinguists have explained the advantages by proposing a so called 'sensitive period' in childhood for language learning. Originally, Eric Lenneberg proposed the Critical Period Hypothesis (CPH) (1967), which suggested that brain plasticity was only conducive to language learning until puberty. Whilst this strong position has been contested, there seems to be some agreement that there is a sensitive period for acquiring a second language. Children who start younger than 11–12 years of age, given advantageous learning circum-stances, such as plenty of input and interaction in an English environment, are more likely to acquire English to native levels without an accent. Immersed children are motivated to be integrated into the language community and this is an important factor in their success.

Is younger better?

On balance, research into the advantages of younger learners, especially in formal non-English environments, is not so conclusively positive. If we compare those who started younger in primary schools with those who started a bit later in secondary school, most studies show that the advantages of the early starters tend to disappear by the time children are 16. In the summary of the European Union's recommendations in 1998 Christiane Blondin and her colleagues caution that younger learners' advantage over older learners seems to be minimal. The advantages concern young children's intuitive grasp of language and their ability to be more attuned to the phono-logical system of the new language. The consensus is that children are sensitive to the sounds and the rhythm of new languages and they enjoy copying new sounds and patterns of intonation. In addition, younger learners are less anxious and less inhibited and, overall, they can spend more time devoted to the language compared with those who start later. In the long term this longer period spent learning may have positive effects.

At the same time this report stresses that older learners use more efficient strategies, have a more mature conceptual world to rely on, have a clearer sense of discourse and, more importantly, have a clearer sense of why they are learning a new language. It seems that the advantages older learners enjoy can ultimately compensate for an early start. Adults and older learners are more analytical and give attention to detail, which helps with language learning. The only area that is difficult to compensate for seems to be pro-nunciation but even here, cultural and identity issues may play a role. Adults and older children might not want to sound English because they want to preserve their own identity. There is another argument which challenges the supposed advantages of an early start. There are some rare but exceptionally successful cases of adults who start learning a second language quite late in life. In his review in 2001 David Singleton, a researcher interested in age in language learning, cites several studies of exceptional adult learners who were mistaken for native speakers by native speaker judges. This means that, with a great deal of dedication, it is possible to learn a second language and to achieve native or near-native levels even in adulthood.

Learning a second language in the playground and at school

From informal to formal contexts

Children's advantages as language learners are most obvious in informal contexts such as in the playground. They tend to pick up language in everyday situations from other children in their environment relatively quickly because they want to play and make friends. Familiar routines and games offer great opportunities for hearing the same language again and again and learning to take part in simple conversations. When children move to another country (for example, a Mexican child to the USA, a Turkish child to Germany, or an Iranian child to the UK), after a short silent period when they are absorbed in listening to input, they can acquire the so-called conversational genre or playground talk fairly quickly. This means that they can communicate, make friends, and function well in everyday conversations as quickly as within the first one or two years of arrival in the new country.

To master the language that is needed for school is quite a different matter. Differences between home language environments and school language environments have already been discussed in the previous chapter. In the case of children who are learning English as a second language, such differences remain relevant. In 2000 a Canadian researcher, Jim Cummins, published a book entitled *Language, Power and Pedagogy: Bilingual Children in the Crossfire*, in which he reviewed research evidence about school second language learning and offered advice to teachers working in contexts where there is a cultural diversity of learners in the same class. He also makes a basic distinction between home language use and school language use. The research summarized by Cummins shows that it takes much longer to catch up with the academic language skills necessary for successful participation in school discourse than with informal conversations. It may take as long as five to seven years before children reach academic levels comparable to those of native speakers of the language. Cummins' findings also suggest that bilingual education can be very beneficial for children with regard to their general development, cognitive, metacognitive, and other skills. One factor which seems important in this process is to develop children's mother tongue and second language literacy skills in parallel rather than neglecting the first language to make way for the second. Respect for their mother tongue and support with their second language are essential. Cummins suggests that educational programmes need to invest a considerable amount of effort into making this process of catching up as rewarding, supportive, and motivating as possible. To help these children, teachers will have to think hard about providing a rich language environment where formal and scientific terms and concepts are carefully introduced and explored, starting with informal concepts and words and phrases that the children are already familiar with. The work of Pauline Gibbons (1995, 2002) in Australia offers a range of practical ideas to teachers interested in managing multicultural classrooms. Gibbons emphasizes the importance of integrating language with content so that language and curriculum knowledge can be developed hand in hand. This means that teachers need to plan explicitly and carefully their language use in class. For example, when teaching children about magnets, it is a good idea to start with language they already have for describing magnetic phenomena, such as 'pull together' or 'pull apart', and then introduce formal terms such as 'attract' and 'repel'. New terms and concepts are introduced with careful attention to both content and language.

Integrated second language learning

In all English-speaking countries there is systematic support available to children who are learning English as their second language in the primary school. Although these children are immersed in a linguistically very rich environment and do receive systematic help and support, research suggests that the process of catching up takes a lot of time, effort, and patience. Rhonda Oliver and her colleagues in Australia, interested in children's second language acquisition, conducted an interesting study in 2003. They investigated the language use of immigrant children who were already proficient in English. These children were considered not to need any more ESL support as they were fully integrated into the curriculum. The study shows that they still had significantly lower levels of acquisition of Australian terms than their native speaker peers. The researchers asked 75 children from five ethnic backgrounds between the ages of eight and 13 to describe pictures of objects that had Australian names. For example, there was a picture of a pedestrian crossing and the children were expected to say it was a crosswalk, which is the appropriate Australian term. The findings showed that when prompted to use specific terms, the immigrant children used generic terms instead or simply indicated that they did not know these words. This study is a good reminder that second language acquisition is a long process and even after many years in the environment, the immigrant children's vocabulary base is different from native children's, for example, in relation to these cultural terms.

Learning English as a foreign language

In many other contexts in the world, however, when children start learning English, they are not immersed in an English environment and they are not learning English to make friends or fit into a new school and culture. They are learning English as a school subject in addition to maths, science, and other timetabled subjects. Compared to the circumstances of a child who is starting a new life abroad, children in non-English environments have limited opportunities to practise the language outside school and no immediate need or clear motivation to use and learn English. On the other hand, both parents and teachers recognize the benefits of learning English and many governments opt for introducing a foreign language into their primary curriculum. Introducing children to a new language offers opportunities to widen their horizons and awaken their early enthusiasm and curiosity about languages.

Summary

In this chapter a variety of circumstances in which children may be learning second languages have been reviewed. These included the advantages of early bilinguals, and the differences between informal and formal immersion contexts. It has been pointed out that younger is not necessarily better when it comes to learning English as a second language, especially if the variables and circumstances are not considered carefully. The next chapter will be devoted to the discussion of factors that ensure that in non-English environments learning English can still be a motivating and worthwhile experience, and children can make good progress in learning to communicate in English.

Recommended reading

Background theory

Cummins, J. 2000. *Language, Power and Pedagogy: Bilingual Children in the Crossfire.* Clevedon: Multilingual Matters.

This book explores the necessary adjustments that need to be made to mainstream curriculum, instruction, and assessment as a result of the fact that many classrooms in the world are becoming culturally and linguistically diverse.

Cunningham-Andersson, U. and **S. Andersson.** 1999. *Growing up with Two Languages: A Practical Guide.* London: Routledge.

This is a book written for teachers and parents who are in contact with children learning more languages. The book is about how to help these children make the most of the benefits of their situation.

Marinova-Todd, S., D. Marshall, and **C. Snow.** 2000. 'Three misconceptions about age and L2 learning.' *TESOL Quarterly* 34/1: 9–34.

This article reviews the evidence for and against starting second language learning at a young age and challenges the folk wisdom that 'younger is necessarily better'.

Singleton, D. and **L. Ryan.** 2004. *Language Acquisition: The Age Factor.* (2nd edition). Clevedon: Multilingual Matters.

This book considers evidence for the age factor in language learning, discussing relevant research in both first and second language acquisition. It contains studies of clinical speech therapy as well as language teaching.

Practical teacher resources

Gibbons, P. 1995. *Learning to Learn in a Second Language.* Merrickwill: Southwood Press Australia.

This book offers a wide range of strategies and activities that teachers working in multilingual classrooms might consider adopting. It covers issues of planning and dealing with both spoken and written language. It advocates a whole school response where the mother tongue is valued and used to the children's advantage.

Gibbons, P. 2002. *Scaffolding Language, Scaffolding Learning: Teaching Second Language Learners in the Mainstream Classroom.* Portsmouth, NH: Heinemann.

This is an excellent source for teachers who are interested in the issues of integrating second language learners into mainstream classrooms. There is a short but very clear introduction to the theory underpinning the principles discussed and demonstrated in the book. Each language skill is considered in detail and many practical activities are offered to try out in classrooms.

Irujo, S. 1998. *Teaching Bilingual Children: A Teacher Resource Book.* London: Heinle & Heinle Publishers.

This book offers interesting insights into a Spanish/English bilingual classroom. There are tasks, classroom extracts, and examples of children's work in addition to the accessible discussion of the theory underlying practice.

Saunders, G. 1983. *Bilingual Children: Guidance for the Family.* Clevedon: Multilingual Matters.

This is the story of the Australian couple who were both native speakers of English but studied German and thus decided to raise their three children bilingual. George Saunders talked to the children only in German while his wife used English. The book is a chronological record of their problems and successes.

Tasks

If you would like to look at some practical tasks to explore your own practice related to the content of this chapter, you can try Task 4: Observing children outside English classes (Appendix page 158).

4 POLICY: PRIMARY ELT PROGRAMMES

Introduction

This chapter will consider how local opportunities and resources can be exploited in order to implement primary foreign language learning programmes with the best possible potential for success. Individual teachers play a key role because their understanding of the benefits and limitations of their own contexts and thus their informed decisions can make a real difference with regard to the success of a particular programme. Understanding variables that influence success is also important to teachers who may be in a position to influence policy decisions. It is important to establish the reasons why primary English language teaching is beneficial and then explore the key factors leading to success.

Contextual factors in language teaching

Language settings

The introduction of any language course or programme, whether it is for adults or children, will be affected by a great number of contextual variables. Behind the language setting of any context there are strong political influences. At the highest level, these influences are associated with the views of the education ministry in a given country on languages in general. This has a knock-on effect on the allocation of funds for training, research programmes, and materials development projects. These political decisions are made in view of the language setting in a particular country. Language setting refers to the totality of language use within a given context. This covers all the languages and their varieties used by speakers in all communities either at home or at work. The language setting includes minority languages, dialects, and second and/or foreign languages. Geographical location also plays a part. For example, in Germany different languages are learnt depending on which country the schools are nearest to. Angelika Kubanek-German (2000), a teacher trainer in Germany, describes so-called

'Border-Programmes'. Within the framework of these programmes, German children close to the borders with France, Italy, the Netherlands, the Czech Republic, and Poland learn the respective languages of these countries. They have the chance to interact with children across the border on a regular basis. They have partner schools and go to summer camps together. These children have the immediate foreign language environment right on their doorstep, which can have a very positive effect on the motivation of both teachers and learners and give them a real sense of purpose.

Educational frameworks

What type of language programme is introduced will also be dependent on the educational framework of the given country. Educational frameworks are vastly different in different countries. In some contexts there is a major divide between primary and secondary schools around the age of ten to 11, while in others primary schooling runs for eight years (from six to 14), divided into a lower primary and upper primary sector. In some countries children start formal schooling at the age of four but in others not until they are six to seven years old. There are also differences in the way the curriculum is structured and the way it is delivered, and these effects may carry over to the introduction of a new language.

Status of English and attitude to English

One very important variable is the status of English in a given country. In some countries it is not used widely in society while in others it enjoys an equal status to the local language. Whatever its status, it is also important to consider both learners' and teachers' attitudes to English. In the case of children these beliefs and attitudes are still malleable. Children of primary school age may not have strong opinions about other cultures or language learning in general even though parental and teacher influences might already have made an impact. Children whose parents speak several languages and move comfortably between cultures will certainly be able to develop positive attitudes and accept different cultures more easily. Children who are brought up in a monolingual environment may meet new cultures and new languages through the experience of a primary foreign language programme. For these children this experience will be of crucial importance in establishing positive attitudes about other cultures and language learning in general.

The role of motivation

In comparison with the first language, motivation is crucial in learning other languages. When we learn our first language, it is all a natural part of growing up. When children move to another country and have to learn a new language, their motivation to learn is related to wanting to fit in with children in their new community. What can be the source of motivation for children in EFL contexts? An interesting study in 1999 by Marianne Nikolov, a Hungarian teacher, trainer, and researcher, shows that children as they get older typically draw on different sources of motivation to learn English. At the beginning, the youngest age groups are motivated by positive attitudes to English and the learning context. This means that they want to learn English because they enjoy the activities and the comfortable atmosphere in class. Very young children also say that they like English because they like the teacher. Young children are therefore intrinsically motivated which means that they want to learn because they enjoy the process of learning English for its own sake. In Nikolov's study extrinsic factors seem to appear later, somewhere around the age of 11 to 12 when children begin to talk about future goals with English, but even at this stage these goals are quite vague and general. Interestingly, in this study the researcher was able to track down the children ten years after the study was completed. She found that all the participants had continued studying and using English and they all evaluated their experience of learning English in the primary school as very positive and valuable.

It is of course very important for teachers to motivate their learners in their English classes. One of the main experts on language learning motivation, Zoltán Dörnyei, in 2001 wrote a practical book for teachers entitled *Motivational Strategies in the Language Classroom* to help them to sustain motivation in their classrooms. This book is not directly for primary teachers only, but the general principles suggested very much apply to all learners and all learning situations. Dörnyei suggests that there are four main components or stages of motivational teaching. The first stage is to create motivating conditions for learning. This means creating a pleasant and supportive environment in the classroom. The next stage is to introduce initial motivational techniques such as talking about values, showing positive attitudes to learning, creating materials that are relevant for the learners, and establishing expectations of success. After this initial stage, teachers need to take care to maintain and protect their learners' motivation by offering stimulating activities and fostering self-esteem, self-confidence, and co-operation among learners. Finally, motivating teachers take care to turn evaluation and feedback into positive experiences. With older children, as part of an ongoing process of protecting motivation, it may be possible to work on self-motivating strategies. Ema Ushioda (1996), another expert on motivation, has written a great deal about this. Self-motivating means to learn and practise techniques that can help learners to think positively about their learning. For example, when children are disappointed by lower test results than expected, it is important for them to evaluate this experience in a constructive way, i.e. they can learn from it and move on to try harder next time.

Aims and expectations

There are many good reasons why primary school children can benefit from foreign language learning. The aims and objectives of primary English programmes usually include the following possibilities:

- Develop children's basic communication abilities in English
- Encourage enjoyment and motivation
- Promote learning about other cultures
- Develop children's cognitive skills
- Develop children's metalinguistic awareness
- Encourage 'learning to learn'.

Most countries tend to emphasize one or both of the first two aims above. The first typically involves teaching children to talk about themselves and their immediate environments, to understand and respond to basic English instructions, and to communicate about topics of interest with a partner. The second main aim is related to the need to make English an attractive school subject to children so as to foster their motivation and encourage them to want to learn languages in the future. At this initial familiarization stage it seems crucial to introduce a foreign language in an enjoyable way. Some contexts may add another dimension such as a cross-cultural aim, and raise learners' awareness about 'otherness' through a different language and thus a different culture. This could include objectives such as learning to take different perspectives, modifying stereotypes, unlearning prejudices, preventing discrimination, and acquiring tolerance. Some contexts may list aims related to cognitive development and/or metalinguistic awareness. It is crucial for teachers to familiarize themselves with the aims and objectives of the programme so that they can set their expectations accordingly. For example, in many contexts linguistic gains in the first few years of primary school will be limited, but there may be substantial gains in increasing language learning motivation and cultural awareness. Parents may often have unrealistic expectations of children's progress and it is a good idea for teachers to make the expectations very clear and transparent.

Exposure to English

How much English children hear and how often they have opportunities to interact in English is a very crucial variable. It is, of course, not possible to achieve in the EFL classroom the levels of exposure found in acquisition rich environments (such as, for example, the immersion classrooms in Canada), but the success of naturalistic learning can be built on. It is important that opportunities are created in the classroom for children to be exposed to natural language and to interact with each other. These factors can have implications for teachers' competencies, both in terms of their proficiency in English to provide the necessary exposure to the language, and of their confidence in methodology to offer opportunities through appropriate tasks and activities for children to communicate with each other in a variety of ways. Teachers' confidence and willingness to use the language naturally in the classroom is a key component of success.

Successful examples such as the 'Croatian project' (a small-scale research project) reported by local teacher trainers Lidvina Stokic and Jelena Djigunovic (2000) demonstrate that timetabling English is crucial. In this project the children start at the age of six to seven and have five lessons a week. They have regular English classes for one hour every day. Such intensity is rewarded with excellent pronunciation and intonation and relatively high levels of proficiency. Another research project conducted in the USA by Helena Curtain (2000) also testified that more intensive foreign language programmes in the primary school resulted in better performance. In this study, English-speaking elementary school children in Spanish programmes were the participants. The children were asked to pass a proficiency test in their fifth grade having completed different courses of different intensity and with different time allocation. Both the test results and the teachers' comments clearly confirmed that the frequency of language lessons was an important factor. When teachers are faced with restrictions of a maximum two to three hours a week, then spreading the lessons out can be a solution. It is better to have 30 minutes every day than just two hours during the whole week. National curriculum guidelines in given contexts will determine the number of hours per week that children will spend learning English but schools can often choose to do more.

Class 3/a	Monday	Tuesday	Wednesday	Thursday	Friday
8:00–8:30	English	English	English	English	English
BREAK					
9:00–9:45	Maths	Reading and writing	Science	Maths	Reading and writing
10:00–10:45	Science	Maths	Reading	Reading and writing	Science
11:00–11:45	Art	Science	Art	Games	Maths
12:00–12:45	P.E.	Music	Games	Music	P.E.

Integrating English into the curriculum

Another question, related to total time and timetabling, is whether the school will follow a programme where English is treated as a separate subject or integrate English as naturally as possible into the existing primary programme. Some countries follow quite rigid subject-based teaching in the primary school and thus English as a separate subject might fit better. In these contexts English is timetabled for about two hours a week and often a specialist teacher from a secondary school comes in to teach the language. Other countries have already opted for an integrated approach where English is carefully embedded into the primary curriculum. In these contexts English is taught by the class teacher. This means that the children have the opportunity to link their knowledge in maths, science, music, or geography with English. Some sort of integration between the rest of the curriculum and the foreign language seems sensible for a great many reasons. For example, if we believe that younger children learn holistically, then it would make sense to integrate English into other learning. Revisiting various concepts and words in a foreign language can reinforce previously taught information. Integration also carries the underlying message that everything can be talked about in both the first and the foreign language. Some contexts advocate only a small amount of integration, for example, at the level of using basic mathematical operations in the foreign language, or using instructions in the PE lesson in English. At a different level, teachers may decide to spend a series of lessons on a topic associated with a particular area of the curriculum. If children are learning about construction materials and types of houses in their geography lesson, there may be opportunities for the English teacher to plan a series of English lessons around the same theme. There are a great many schools in many contexts where English is used across the curriculum in a systematic way throughout the primary years. In these schools the term 'Content and Language Integrated Learning' (CLIL) is often used. This is very similar to the approach of integrating language and content in multilingual classrooms in that both content and language are developed simultaneously. For example, in Finland children start English at the age of nine and have a gradual increase of English throughout their primary school. There are many opportunities to link English with other aspects of the curriculum, such as geography, arts, maths, and physical education (PE), and by the end of primary school children may end up using English almost as often as their mother tongue.

It is often assumed that integrated teaching or content-based teaching is associated with large amounts of ongoing contact hours because it is not possible to engage students whose proficiency is not sufficiently advanced in meaningful content relevant activities. However, an interesting study in the USA found that this was not the case. Jingzi Huang, a Chinese researcher, conducted a study in 2003 with children aged nine to 11 enrolled in a Chinese as a foreign language programme in the USA. These children were learning Chinese in just two hours per week and did not have Chinese-speaking relatives to practise with outside school. Despite these limitations, the teachers decided to implement a content driven programme. This meant that the cultural content was first planned and language emerged from meaningful cultural topics such as comparing the daily routines of Chinese and American children of similar ages. In this study the children found content driven teaching motivating and satisfying, and with the use of good visuals and other supporting materials, the learners even at the near beginners' level were able to communicate with each other and learn new content through the target language. This research study may inspire other teachers working with lower level classes of children to explore the opportunities of content-based teaching.

Teacher factors

For the successful introduction of English into primary schools in any one country, the government needs to invest in recruiting and training teachers. This applies to both pre-service and in-service teacher training and opportunities for teachers for development. Many countries run well established primary English teacher training courses. However, many countries face a difficult situation with a critical shortage of qualified teachers.

The primary class teacher who delivers the rest of the curriculum and who has a good knowledge of the children as well as the language is in the best position to succeed. Knowledge of the curriculum means that class teachers can integrate English easily and naturally into the day. Class teachers know the children and their special needs, such as a safe and encouraging environment, stimulation, fun, and variety as well as plenty of recycling. Finally, primary English teachers need to have adequate proficiency in the language to provide comprehensible input and natural exposure to the target language. An interesting survey by a Japanese researcher in America, Yuko Goto Butler (2004), explored primary English teachers' own perceptions of their proficiency. She compared the opinions of primary English teachers from three Asian countries: Korea, Japan, and Taiwan. To the question of whether they saw their own proficiency level as adequate to teach the curriculum effectively, all answered that they felt they fell below the necessary level of competence. They identified spoken competence as the area of most concern. Yuko Goto Butler suggests that it is important to explore further just what proficiency levels are needed in primary schools and how teachers could be supported. Many teachers may lack confidence in their own proficiency but with constant practice and good supplementary materials (such as tapes) they can both manage and improve.

Continuity and the private sector

By continuity we mean an opportunity for children to continue their language learning at secondary level by building on the knowledge brought over from primary school. As early as 1974, the 'Burstall Report' on the evaluation of the ten-year pilot primary French teaching in England and Wales identified the transition from primary to secondary school as one of the shortcomings of the programme. Interestingly, continuity still remains one of the major challenges of the implementation of successful primary programmes. In their edited collection of papers describing TEYL programmes in 18 countries (Europe and beyond), Marianne Nikolov and Helena Curtain (2000) identify lack of continuity as the major obstacle to success. In many contexts, there is no agreed outcome associated with primary programmes and children from different primary schools may have been taught very different things from very different books. This is why many secondary programmes decide to start again from the beginning. This can have a negative effect on learners' motivation levels and will present additional challenges for teachers in secondary schools.

In many countries there is also a thriving private sector of language schools for young learners. These private language schools often run parallel to state primary English programmes. Many children attend private schools where they learn English on top of the regular classes at school. Parents believe that attending two courses will be more effective in the long run. Both parents and children are attracted by intensive summer courses and the English-only policy in these private schools where children are often taught by native speakers. These programmes could be even more effective if they could build on children's English learning in state schools.

Summary

When they decide to introduce TEYL programmes, local governments and authorities need to consider issues such as the characteristics of their educational system and how far the primary curriculum can be integrated with English, and how much they can afford to spend on teacher education and ensuring continuity between primary and secondary language learning. Whatever decisions are made, however, class teachers with suitable methodology and a good command of the language are the most essential components of success. The teacher is also the main source of motivation for many young children.

Recommended reading

Background theory

Blondin, C., M. Candelier, P. Edelenbos, R. Johnstone, A. Kubanek-German, and **T. Taeschner.** 1998. *Foreign Language in Primary and Pre-school Education: a Review of Recent Research within the European Union.* London: Centre for Information on Language Teaching.

This is a comprehensive review of European research into the teaching and learning of modern languages in the pre-primary and primary sectors. It offers a list of conditions that lead to success with primary language programmes in the form of useful recommendations which are applicable in many other contexts outside Europe.

Gilbert, I. 2003 *Essential Motivation in the Classroom.* London and New York: RoutledgeFalmer: Taylor and Francis Group.

This is an easy-to-read book full of anecdotes about motivation and effective teaching and learning. The author offers strategies, ideas, and insights to encourage all teachers of all levels to be inspired to be more motivating and foster their learners' motivation from within.

Nikolov, M. and **H. Curtain.** 2000. *An Early Start: Young Learners and Modern Languages in Europe and Beyond.* Strasbourg: Council of Europe Publishing.

This book offers a description of language programmes in the primary sector in 18 contexts in Europe and beyond. Contexts in Europe are fully covered and countries outside Europe include examples from Australia, Canada, the USA, and Hong Kong. The descriptions offer detailed information about the learners, the teachers, and the educational systems of each country together with the challenges and problems that early language programmes face.

Practical teacher resources

Doyé, P. 1999. *The Intercultural Dimension: Foreign Language Education in the Primary School.* Berlin: Cornelsen Verlag.

This book explores both theory and related practical ideas in the area of intercultural understanding. This concept includes teaching children about 'otherness' and developing an open attitude to new cultures.

Tierney, D. and **M. Hope.** 1998. *Making the Link: Relating Languages to Other Work in the School: Young Pathfinder 7.* London: CILT.

The CILT series for primary language teachers is a practical series full of ideas for classroom use. The examples for learner activities are explained in

English but they are originally designed for learning other languages such as Spanish, French, or German. This particular book offers many good ideas for linking areas of the primary curriculum with language learning. Themes include examples such as 'Around the school' or 'Villages'. There is a special chapter on ideas to exploit festivals.

Rixon, S. 2000. 'Optimum age or optimum conditions? Issues related to the teaching of languages to primary age children' *http://www.britcoun.org/english/eyl/articele01.htm*. British Council.

This is an article which discusses factors of successful TEYL programmes. Shelagh Rixon, in co-operation with the British Council, has created a database at the above website which provides frequently updated information about TEYL programmes in many countries of the world.

Tasks

If you would like to look at some practical tasks to explore your own practice related to the content of this chapter, you can try Task 5: 'Exploring teaching and learning contexts' (Appendix page 158).

5 TEACHING LISTENING AND SPEAKING

Introduction

It was suggested in the previous chapter that the teacher was a key player in the overall success of TEYL programmes and one of the reasons why this is the case is because teachers are the major sources of language input for children. Just as in mother tongue learning, English should start with an emphasis on listening and then speaking. These are the two main skills to teach first because children often cannot read and write at all yet, or not with much confidence. Young beginners need to start with plenty of listening practice, and opportunities to listen to rich input will naturally lead to speaking tasks. In this way, listening and speaking are truly integrated in the primary English classroom.

Teaching listening

Children in an English as a foreign language class will listen to a great variety of texts but above all to their teacher: talking, singing, chanting, dramatizing dialogues, giving instructions, and telling stories. Although in the early stages the teacher will remain their main source of listening input, children might also listen to video and audio tapes especially if these come with the coursebook the teacher is using. Teachers can be supported with good quality tapes to accompany their teaching if they are not yet confident about their own language proficiency.

Listening—aspects of difficulty

Listening is an active skill and there are many factors that contribute to its difficulty. It is important in the early stages to avoid these sources of difficulty and introduce them only gradually. One source of difficulty is the type and length of the text the children listen to. Another factor is the familiarity of the person who they are listening to. It is easier to listen to the teacher than to recordings because teachers can adjust the speed of their speech and modify their language. The teacher can also repeat messages and use gestures and facial expressions to help children to work out the meaning. What also makes a difference is the response the children need to make before, while, or after they listen.

There are two basic sub-skills that competent and mature listeners use all the time. One set of sub-skills is referred to as 'bottom-up' skills. These help learners build up the language from constituent parts. Relying on their knowledge of the linguistic system, listeners use bottom-up skills to segment the speech they hear and make sense of it. Knowing the language system helps learners to work out, for example, what the unstressed grammar words are in a particular sentence even without hearing or listening out for every word. Speakers of all ages find this processing difficult but children will have particular difficulties. Depending on their age and the type of teaching they have been exposed to, they may not know much about the abstract rule system of English and therefore they may lack the ability to manipulate the system from bottom up. Parallel with 'bottom-up' processing, successful listeners also do simultaneous 'top-down' processing. They rely on their schematic knowledge, i.e. their mental frameworks for various topics and their world knowledge to fill in gaps in their understanding, make guesses and interpretations as they follow the listening text. In comparison with adults, children have less developed schematic knowledge about many topics; they know less about the world in general and therefore guess and infer meaning with more difficulty. The younger the children, the more this applies.

Support with listening

In order to support children with both bottom-up and top-down work, teachers may want to focus on giving them listening tasks that are meaning driven and help them to develop these strategies slowly. In order to support top-down processing, teachers can make sure that listening is carefully embedded in the here-and-now context of familiar games and routines such as stories and action rhymes so that children do not need to infer the context or topic for themselves. Gestures and visuals will help, too. With regard to bottom-up processing, it is important that children are given tasks that do not require them to manipulate linguistic features that they do not know yet and are not interested in, such as translating, analysing constituent parts of phrases and sentences, and substituting patterns. Instead, children should start with easier 'listen and do' activities. Many coursebook activities ask children to 'listen and read', meaning that they can follow the text on the page as they listen, which helps with bottom-up processing. This, of course, is only helpful if they can read.

Teacher talk in the primary English lesson

In young learners' classrooms, especially at the beginning stages of learning a language, teachers often talk a lot in the target language because they provide the language input. This helps children to get used to the intonation patterns and the sounds of the language. Teachers talk and comment on what is going on as they point to pictures in the book or on the classroom wall, or as they mime something (see Figure 5.1).

As children listen, they are engaged in working out what is going on and for some of the time they may choose to remain silent and just absorb the

Figure 5.1: Examples of teacher talk

language. This is similar to the first couple of years in learning the mother tongue. Of course, they do not necessarily understand every word the teacher says but most children will be able to work out the meaning from the context, the gestures, and the visual aids. When teachers use English (the target language) to give instructions, tell a story, or introduce a song or a rhyme, children who have just started learning may comment in their mother tongue on what they think is happening because they cannot yet contribute in the second language. The teacher may want to accept children's comments in their first language and also encourage them by confirming their guesses and contributions, and incorporating their utterances into the target language. There is also an important social, affective function of teacher talk. Teachers will use a lot of praise and encouragement and will model social conventions such as saying hello at the beginning of the lesson.

Interactional modifications of language

During interactions of any kind between adults or children in any language, there are inevitably communication breakdowns. This simply means that the partners do not always understand what the other has just said. When a breakdown or misunderstanding is judged by the speakers as unimportant, they might simply ignore it and just carry on talking. However, if the breakdown is serious, the conversational partners will decide to repair and rephrase what has been said by modifying their original language use. This is often referred to as 'language modification'. Modifying language to avoid and solve misunderstandings can include using repetitions, comprehension checks ('Do you understand what I am trying to say?'), clarification requests ('What did you say?'), and confirmation checks ('Did you say you got five?'). Michael Long, a linguist in America, and many of his colleagues conducted research studies in the 1980s with adult EFL learners to explore interactional modifications, and found that the processes of negotiating meaning (modifying language and asking for modifications from a partner) facilitated second language acquisition (Long 1983).

Almost all empirical research in this area has however been conducted with adults. One study that stands out because it was conducted with children and in an EFL setting has interesting supportive evidence. This study was carried out in Spain with ten-year-old children. In 2001 Marcos Peñate Cabrera and Plácido Bazo Martínez investigated the effects of two types of story input in their English classes. One story was told to the children using simplified sentence structures and vocabulary, but without repetitions, comprehension checks, and supporting gestures (interactional modifications). The other story was told using the original story text with interactional modifications. The children's understanding was measured afterwards using a comprehension test. The results showed that the groups of children who heard the story with interactive modifications understood and recalled the story significantly better. The children were also asked in an interview for their opinion about which type of storytelling was easier to understand. All the children considered that listening with interactive modifications was easier. In addition to the linguistic features, the authors of this study also stressed the importance of using gestures as 'tools' to assist input.

To illustrate how teachers can modify their language and make messages more accessible to children, Table 5.1 gives an example of a teacher's modifications to the story of the 'Fat Cat' (see page 52).

Once upon a time there was an old, old woman. How old is she? Is she 50, 60, or 70? What do you think? Yes, I think she is 70 or 80 years old. Very old. Look at the picture. What is this? What did she have? She had a what? Yes, she had a cat. Yes, cat. Is this is a thin cat or a fat cat? Yes, a fat cat. A fat cat (gesture). A black cat. Do you like the cat? Hm, one day, the old lady made some soup for lunch. Look, here is the pot. There is soup in the pot. Hmm, lovely soup. The old lady said to the cat, 'Cat, watch the soup in the pot. I must go to my sister.' The cat said, 'Don't worry. I will watch the soup.' So the old woman went to her sister. What do you think the cat did when the old woman left (repeat question in first language)? Let's see. Oh, look, the cat is eating. The cat ate the soup. And what else? And ate the pot, too. Oh, no. Look how big he is now. I think he is very hungry, hungry (gesture). He ate the soup and the pot too.

Table 5:1 Extract from a story modification (from The Fat Cat *by J. Kent, Puffin 1974)*

We can see how the teacher elicits information from the children, builds on what they already know, comments on the story, and keeps children engaged by asking them to predict what will happen next. She also makes use of the illustrations which help learners follow the storyline. She repeats language for emphasis and uses examples to highlight concepts, and she modifies language by offering alternatives and synonyms. Such input can be a very rich source of language learning and also serves as meaningful practice in listening.

Listening activities for younger learners

Where do we start with younger learners? In order to give children plenty of listening practice and help them tune into English, many young learners' coursebooks and resource books initially recommend mainly activities which require nonverbal responses from children. One such task is to listen to rhymes or action stories or songs and enjoy them by miming the actions rather than immediately producing the language. The nonverbal contributions help make sense of the content. The important principle is that children have the opportunity to absorb the language before they have to say anything. Such responses to listening are associated with Total Physical Response (TPR), an approach to language learning originally developed in the 1960s in America. TPR links learning to physical actions and ensures that learners will hear a lot of natural English in meaningful contexts without having to respond verbally. The example in Extract 1 is taken from *Buzz 1*.

Extract 1 (Revell, Seligson, and Wright 1995)

The instructions in the Teacher's book are as follows:
• The teacher does the actions as the cassette is played;
• Pupils join in as they become confident;
• Pupils point to pictures in the book as they hear the instructions;
• Pupils do the actions and join in with the words if they want.

The new language is introduced with support from the teachers' gestures and the illustrations in the book. These help children grasp the meaning. There are two different nonverbal responses recommended here. First, children join in with the actions, then point to the pictures. Even at the stage of language production, it is emphasized in the teacher's book that this should be optional. Eventually most children probably want to join in and say the rhyme. Most coursebooks contain rhymes, songs, and action stories which can be used in this way. There are also resource books in which teachers can find additional materials, and some confident and creative teachers may feel inspired to write their own. (See more about this in Chapter 9.)

A great deal of listening practice in the early years can grow out of TPR. For example, there are the so-called 'listen and respond' games such as 'listen and clap your hands', or 'Simon says'. In these activities children have to listen and understand messages, decide whether they are right or wrong, and act accordingly. Other activities such as 'Listen and draw the picture' or 'Listen and colour in the clown's clothes' include drawing or colouring. Yet other exercises include simple ticking or circling or require some writing, such as true and false. Many of these are focused 'listen and do' exercises with an end product such as a picture, a colourful clown, or an animal mask to take home to show parents. Because of the focused nature of these tasks, it is easy for the teacher to monitor what children have understood from the listening text. These activities not only give excellent listening practice but also offer opportunities for incorporating into the English class multiple intelligences through sticking, colouring, and making simple objects. (See more about this in Chapter 1.)

The typical 'listen and do' activity in Extract 2, for the younger age group, is taken from *New English Parade Starter B*. It is a simple 'listen and colour' activity where children colour their fish and then glue them into the fish bowl.

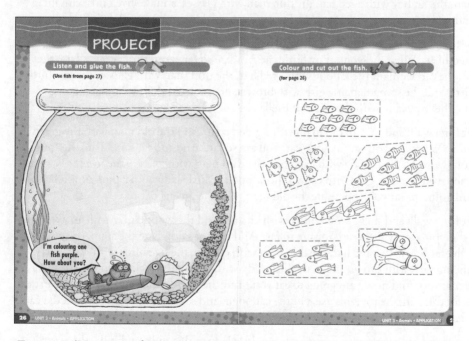

Extract 2 (Herrera and Zanatta 2001a)

Listening to stories is the most authentic and popular activity for all children, and primary English teachers can use storytelling as additional listening practice. Children will learn new language as well as having

An old woman lived with her cat in her house. She made soup for lunch and she said, 'Cat, watch the soup in the pot. I must go to my sister.' The cat said to her, 'OK. Don't worry. I will watch the soup in the pot.' But when the old woman went out, the cat ate all the soup. And the pot, too. When the old lady came back, she asked the cat, 'What happened to the soup and the pot?' 'Oh,' said the cat, 'I ate the soup and the pot too. And now I am going to eat you.' And he ate the old woman too.

The cat went for a walk. And he met a fat boy with a red hat. And the fat boy asked him, 'What did you eat my little cat? You are so fat.' And the cat said, 'I ate the soup, the pot, and the old woman too. And now I am going to eat you.' So he ate the fat boy with the red hat too.

The cat went for a walk. And he met a thin man with glasses. And the thin man asked him, 'What did you eat my little cat? You are so fat.' And the cat said, 'I ate the soup, the pot, the old woman, and the fat boy with a red hat too. And now I am going to eat you.' So he ate the thin man with glasses too.

The cat went for a walk and met five birds with nice shirts. And the five birds asked him, 'What did you eat my little cat? You are so fat.' And the cat said, 'I ate the soup, the pot, the old woman, the fat boy with a red hat, and the thin man with glasses too. And now I am going to eat you.' So he ate the five birds with nice shirts too.

The cat went for a walk and met seven dancing girls with brown shoes. And the seven dancing girls asked him, 'What did you eat my little cat? You are so fat.' And the cat said, 'I ate the soup, the pot, the old woman, the fat boy with a red hat, the thin man with glasses, and the five birds with nice shirts too. And now I am going to eat you.' So he ate the seven dancing girls with brown shoes too.

The cat went for a walk and met a little lady with a pink umbrella. And the little lady with a pink umbrella asked him, 'What did you eat my little cat? You are so fat.' And the cat said, 'I ate the soup, the pot, the old woman, the fat boy with a red hat, the thin man with glasses, the five birds with nice shirts, and the seven dancing girls with brown shoes too. And now I am going to eat you.' So he ate the little lady with the pink umbrella too.

The cat went for a walk and met an old man with a green coat. And the old man with the green coat asked him, 'What did you eat my little cat? You are so fat.' And the cat said, 'I ate the soup, the pot, the old woman, the fat boy with a red hat, the thin man with glasses, the five birds with nice shirts, the seven dancing girls with brown shoes, and the little lady with a pink umbrella too. And now I am going to eat you.' So he ate the old man with the green coat too.

The cat went for a walk and met a woodcutter with an axe. And the woodcutter with an axe asked him, 'What did you eat my little cat? You are so fat.' And the cat said: 'I ate the soup, the pot, the old woman, the fat boy with a red hat, the thin man with glasses, the five birds with nice shirts, the seven dancing girls with brown shoes, the little lady with a pink umbrella, and the old man with a green coat too. And now I am going to eat you.' But the woodcutter said, 'No, you can't eat me, my little fat cat.' And he took his axe, cut the cat open, and saved everybody. He told the cat not to be greedy any more.

And out jumped the old man with a green coat, the little lady with a pink umbrella, the seven dancing girls with brown shoes, the five birds with nice shirts, the thin man with glasses, the fat boy with the red hat, and the old woman with her soup in the pot.

So the woman took her soup and went home. This is the end of the story.

Extract 3 The story of the Fat Cat (Kent 1974)

enjoyable listening practice. Language is picked up easily because stories contain repetition which makes linguistic input more noticeable. Songs, rhymes, and stories often use repetition to make the input salient in this way. In the following story there are many types of repetitive patterns which make new language stand out. The example in Extract 3 is a Danish folk tale which has variations in many other cultures.

This is a 'cumulative repetitive' story. There is a pattern to what happens to nearly everybody who meets the fat cat. The dialogue between the cat and the other characters also follows a clear pattern. Each character is introduced with a similar phrase i.e. noun +with + adjective + noun: 'a girl with brown shoes'. Every time a new character is introduced, the cat repeats the same phrase adding another animal or person. This is like a chain memory practice for vocabulary. These patterns will be picked up by the children without much effort because they are so salient in the input. Predictability will enhance understanding. Visuals, i.e. the pictures in the book, gestures, and interactive modifications will also help. Children will find they want to join in with parts of the story. Chanting together means that individual contributions are voluntary and safe. Those children who are not ready can just listen. In addition to the listening practice, the recurring linguistic patterns in the dialogue between the cat and the other characters can be developed as a model for follow-up speaking practice. Initially controlled dialogues and drill-like repetition can lead to freer dramatization or role-plays. Listening to stories, rhymes, and songs can also lead to learning the words and phrases by heart and this can be very useful because songs and rhymes contain reasonably fast connected speech in English, with shortened sounds and the use of 'schwa' [ə], such as in 'cutter' [kʌtə].

Listening activities for older learners

The majority of the activities in the previous section can be used with older learners as well especially at the beginning stages. For example, 'Simon says' works with older learners as well. Perhaps the instructions themselves might become more challenging. Older learners also enjoy storytelling but the teacher will have to make careful judgements about the type of story that is suitable. It is possible to look for longer stories or stories from other cultures. With older learners, it is a good idea to introduce tapes rather than just the teacher's input because children will have to get used to faster speech, un-familiar speakers, and different accents. It is possible to increase difficulty by varying text length and activity types. Activities used with younger learners can be adapted for older ones by increasing the level of difficulty. For example, within the category of 'listen and do' it is possible to introduce activities which require quite a lot of processing, such as 'listen and identify one person', where the learners have to listen to a passage and work out which person is being described. The more people there are to choose from, the more difficult the task is. Task difficulty therefore is largely dependent on the kind of output required. Younger learners may be asked to join in with a story while older learners can rewrite the story ending and act it out.

As children grow older, they get better at both bottom-up and top-down processing. They learn more both about the linguistic system and about the world around them, which makes predictions and guessing more reliable. They can also alternate between these two skills depending on the task at hand. In Extract 4, taken from *New English Parade 6,* children listen to a recording of a professor talking about the future. They read and understand the four sentences from the book to focus their attention. The task is to decide which of these sentences they hear in the listening text.

Extract 4 (Herrera and Zanatta 2001b)

Extract 5, taken from *Tip Top 4,* illustrates how older learners can begin to use their predicting skills to make certain assumptions about the content of the listening before they hear it. First of all, children can look at the photos of the four readers and guess what they may be collecting. Then they listen and find out whether their predictions were right. When they listen the third time, they focus on other parts of the text. They listen for specific detail about the reasons why different children wanted to collect different things.

This example illustrates that older learners can use their predicting skills to their advantage. The text is a rich source for practice, through getting the learners to focus on different aspects of the text each time. It is also important to add that texts like this illustrate well that it is not necessary to understand every single word. As long as the learners can complete the task, the listening has been useful and successful. Teachers can explicitly focus on helping children to be aware of useful listening skills. (See more about this in Chapter 8.)

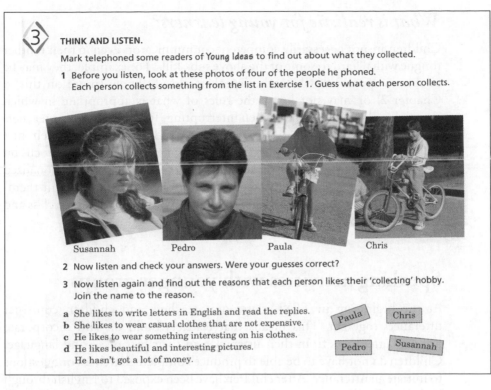

THINK AND LISTEN.

Mark telephoned some readers of Young Ideas to find out about what they collected.

1 Before you listen, look at these photos of four of the people he phoned.
   Each person collects something from the list in Exercise 1. Guess what each person collects.

Susannah   Pedro   Paula   Chris

2 Now listen and check your answers. Were your guesses correct?

3 Now listen again and find out the reasons that each person likes their 'collecting' hobby.
  Join the name to the reason.

a She likes to write letters in English and read the replies.
b She likes to wear casual clothes that are not expensive.
c He likes to wear something interesting on his clothes.
d He likes beautiful and interesting pictures.
  He hasn't got a lot of money.

Paula   Chris
Pedro   Susannah

Extract 5 (Rixon 1993)

Teaching speaking

Fluent speakers

Learning to speak fluently and accurately is one of the greatest challenges for all language learners. This is because to be able to speak fluently, we have to speak and think at the same time. As we speak, we have to monitor our output and correct any mistakes, as well as planning for what we are going to say next. To be able to speak fluently in a foreign language requires a lot of practice. Speaking practice starts with practising and drilling set phrases and repeating models. A great deal of time in language classrooms is often spent on these repetitive exercises. Speaking practice, however, can also mean communicating with others in situations where spontaneous contributions are required. Fluent speakers will also have to learn a range of other things such as what is appropriate to say in certain situations, how to manage conversations, and how to interrupt and offer their own contributions. It is a difficult and lengthy process to master all these sub-skills.

What is realistic for young learners?

Children are not necessarily competent communicators even in their mother tongue with regard to some of the above sub-skills. For example, they may be unable to appreciate what other speakers already know (more on this in Chapter 2) or may not know the rules of what is appropriate in which situation or how to be polite when interrupting. It is important for teachers to familiarize themselves with what their children can do in their first language. At the beginning stages with children it is a good idea to focus on simple but purposeful and meaningful pattern drilling and personalized dialogue building in order to prepare them to be able to talk about themselves and their world and to begin to interact with their friends in class and other speakers of the language.

Speaking activities with younger groups

At the beginning in TEYL classrooms teachers and children construct utterances together. This means that teachers build on and incorporate learners' utterances from their utterances in their first or second language. Children do not have to be able to produce complete sentences or questions to initiate an utterance. After children have been exposed to English through listening, they soon want and are able to participate in interactions with the teacher and each other. Many children will want to start copying simple phrases, join in with rhymes and songs, answer simple questions, introduce themselves, and memorize short dialogues. The first building blocks that allow children to move from listening to speaking and to begin to participate in interactions with others are so-called 'unanalysed chunks'. This means that children can remember phrases from previously heard input and use them without conscious analysis. Chunks will often be learnt from the teacher's input or from other texts such as songs, rhymes, chants, stories, and dialogues. For example, if the teacher says, 'See you tomorrow' at the end of every lesson, some learners will pick this up and learn it as an unanalysed chunk. They may understand that it is like saying goodbye because the teacher always says it at the end of the lesson but they will not be able to articulate, for example, that the phrase consists of three words, or what each word means in isolation.

All speakers of English use chunks. Some chunks are fixed while others can be complemented. Fully fixed chunks such as 'see you later' 'what a surprise', or 'what do you think' are complete and ready to use. Partially fixed chunks, such as the chunk 'have you got', are those which require additional elements. Chunks help speakers to produce language faster because they do not have to think of the individual words. Children use more chunks than adults do because they do not share adults' tendency to analyse language into constituent parts. Chunks will be picked up effortlessly by the children but teachers can also explicitly choose to teach set phrases as chunks as in the following example:

A <What do you like>?
B <I like> pizza.
A <What do you like>?
C <I like> chicken.

This mini-dialogue, for example, contains a fixed chunk <What do you like> that teachers can present and practise as a whole. The other chunk is a partially fixed one <I like>, which the children can begin to complete by substituting the original dialogue with items that are personally relevant. These dialogues are quite limited and drill-like at the beginning so it is essential that such practice is fun and as meaningful and purposeful as possible. Here is an example of how to make drilling fun. Guessing games, though fun, are usually drill-like. For example, one child comes to the front of the classroom and mimes an animal. The rest of the class ask questions, 'Are you a monkey? Are you a giraffe?' All their questions follow the same pattern. However, the purpose of the activity is meaningful to them. It is a guessing game and whoever guesses the right answer gets to come out and mime another animal.

Many other language games which are enjoyed in foreign language classrooms require such repetitive contributions. For example, 'I spy', 'What's the time, Mr Wolf?', 'I went to the market and got some apples, bananas, and pears ...'. These activities give children a sense of security and confidence which in turn might increase their motivation levels. In these activities children often copy an original text and use it as a model to create their own. Extract 6 is taken from *Zabadoo 3*.

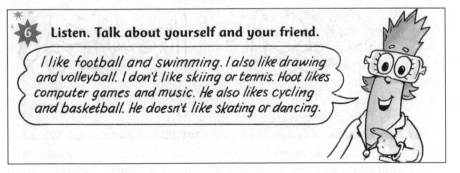

6 **Listen. Talk about yourself and your friend.**

I like football and swimming. I also like drawing and volleyball. I don't like skiing or tennis. Hoot likes computer games and music. He also likes cycling and basketball. He doesn't like skating or dancing.

Extract 6 (Davies 2002)

In this exercise the children are encouraged to listen to or read a 'model' which they then personalize by creating their own description of what they and their friends like doing. They are supported by this model as to how much to say, how to construct the sentences, and what kind of activities to mention. It is meaningful in that the children have a choice of what to substitute in the model patterns. This type of exercise can lead to simple surveys where each member of the class is asked the same question and the results are displayed. For example, following on from the previous activity, the children could ask each other what they like and don't like doing and thus find out what is the most popular activity in their class. In large classes this can be carried out in groups. The advantage is that this practice is personalized and gives everybody a chance to talk. Table 5.2 shows the results of a survey.

Swimming	Tennis	Basketball	Singing	Dancing	Acting	Riding	Other
Jasleen	Yes	No	No	Yes	Yes	Yes	No
Bethany	No	No	No	Yes	Yes	Yes	Yes
Sylvia	Yes	Yes	No	Yes	Yes	No	No
Mark	Yes	Yes	Yes	No	Yes	No	Yes
Tom	Yes	Yes	Yes	Yes	No	No	No
Louise	Yes	No	Yes	No	Yes	Yes	Yes
Others							

Table 5:2 A survey of pastimes

Speaking activities with older learners

Many of the simple dialogues or drills can of course be used with older learners. Dialogues can also lead to interviews or role-play which may require some spontaneous, creative language use. Children will also have to learn how to manage more complex tasks. In order to use such tasks in classrooms, teachers may have to prepare learners. First of all, it is important to teach children phrases which allow them to check what they did not hear or cannot make sense of (for example, 'Sorry, I did not understand. What did you say?'). Teachers can equip learners with useful classroom language such as 'It is your turn', 'Give me the dice', 'Which one is mine?', 'What have you got?' to manage interactive games and tasks. Such language can be displayed on posters. Some of the tasks might require that the learners pay attention to what their partner is saying, ask for and give clarification, repair a communication breakdown, or express themselves explicitly, with extra care. This is all part of 'learning to learn' (see Chapter 8).

Need for meaning negotiation

During games and interactive tasks learners often have to negotiate meaning, i.e. make sure that they understand each other. Research shows that children's ability to negotiate meaning when they do not understand something grows gradually with age and older learners can successfully repair conversations. Younger children, however, cannot reliably take responsibility for clarifying things in conversations. Rod Ellis and Rick Heimbach in 1997 investigated younger children's ability to negotiate meaning in situations when they did not understand new words. Ten kindergarten children were asked to participate in a small-scale study in an ESL programme in an American school in Japan. The children were five or six years old. In a pre-test the researchers established what vocabulary the children did not know and these words were selected for the purposes of the study. An experienced ESL teacher practised a listening task with individuals and groups using the new words. The children had to pretend to be zookeepers, listen to some instructions, and place a bug or a bird in the correct cage on the board. The teacher was a helper who would answer any questions the zookeepers had. The teacher did the task with individual children, making it clear that if they did not understand any of the instructions they could ask for help. Ellis and Heimbach found that there was a great deal of difference in individual children's preparedness or ability to negotiate. Overall the results showed that instead of negotiating the meaning of new words, the children used guesswork when faced with uncertainty.

Older children in Australia in Rhonda Oliver's study in 1998 were found to negotiate meaning more successfully. Two tasks were selected from commercially used materials. In the first task the children described simple black outline objects for their partners to draw. In the second task, which was of jigsaw format, each participant had an outline of a kitchen with cut-out items to be placed in it. The children in the study were between the ages of eight and 13. 128 non-native speaker and 64 native speaker children participated. Oliver found that all the children in her study negotiated meaning. However, when comparing their use of these strategies with that of adults, Oliver found that they used meaning negotiation strategies in a different proportion. They focused on constructing their own meaning rather than facilitating their partners' meaning. As a result, they used more clarification checks, confirmation checks, and repetition but not comprehension checks. So, while the children were mainly concerned with their own understanding, the adults tended to be concerned about the needs of their listeners, too.

Oliver suggested that her findings might be influenced by children's developmental level. The implication of these two studies for teachers is that tasks that require meaning negotiation may have to be introduced slowly and carefully, making sure that children are ready and capable of dealing with the demands of the tasks.

The demands of more complex tasks

Information gap tasks, where participants A and B have different information, often require that children say things creatively on the spot and describe details of visuals to each other with some precision. They might have to initiate questions and volunteer information as well as responding to their partners' questions appropriately. They also require that children learn to pay attention to what their partner is saying, check understanding, clarify meaning, and monitor the progression of the task carefully. For example, in Extract 7 on page 62, taken from *Story Magic 3*, one learner has to explain a route to his or her partner. The speaker needs to give clear directions. The listener needs to ask if anything is not clear and then the speaker will have to repeat or paraphrase their message. In this example, A and B speakers share a map so they can use their hands to guide each other on the map. This activity also requires an understanding of maps and thus a certain level of abstraction.

Information gap tasks, discussion tasks, and other complex speaking tasks can hide various difficulties. It is important for teachers to explore these difficulties with their children and provide plenty of practice of new task types. In my own research (Pinter 2001) I found that even children at the age of ten needed a great deal of practice to be able to deal with the difficulties of two classic information gap tasks: 'Spot the differences' and 'Follow the route on the map'.

Table 5.3 summarizes the most common difficulties and provides simple examples.

It is important for teachers to exercise their best judgement when selecting tasks for older and more experienced learners because tasks need to be motivating but not too difficult. Creating a positive learning environment can certainly help. Children will speak up and contribute to the lesson if they feel happy and secure. It is also crucial that children understand that they can speak up even when they are not sure about their contributions or have only a fragmented answer or idea to offer. This principle has important implications for careful error correction and plenty of encouragement. Children also need purposeful activities which create a communicative need and fuel their motivation to listen and speak. It is often a good idea to talk to children in their first language about the importance of practice in speaking. Teachers may want to encourage practising at home with parents and

Demands	Definition	Example
1 **Linguistic**	Aspects of difficulty such as what type of language is required by a particular task and to what extent the learners can select the linguistic forms they wish to use.	In a picture description task the learner is free to use 'I can see', 'I have got', 'In my picture there is', etc. without any restriction. Can the learners choose? Should the teacher model the language?
2 **Referential**	The need to establish unambiguously what the other person knows or has got.	When learners reconstruct a picture from two incomplete versions, they need to establish first what parts they share. They need safe reference points to refer back to as they build the picture together. Can they establish these safe points? Have they got the English to do this?
3 **Cognitive**	Demands related to attention, memory, and reasoning limitations. Logical or mathematical operations needed.	The game called 'Complete a list of clock faces or numbers' (by discovering the rule) or playing 'noughts and crosses' in teams both require adhering to some rules of logic. Can the children play these games in their first language?
4 **Metacognitive**	Demands which refer to the need in a task or a game to monitor own performance closely while carrying out the task.	Decide to change tactics midway in a noughts and crosses game depending on which squares the other team takes. Can they play this in their first language?
5 **Interactional**	Demands which refer to aspects of turn taking i.e. whether it is obligatory or not in a particular task, conversational management skills, or meaning negotiation.	The need to double-check confusing instructions on a map task by using meaning negotiation moves such as clarification requests.

Table 5.3: Demands in interactive tasks

siblings. Teachers may also want to advise parents about how to help their children, for example, parents can listen to songs, rhymes, and chants, practise dialogues, and encourage any discussion about English.

Extract 7 (House and Scott 2003b)

Summary

Listening and speaking are the two most important skills in most TEYL programmes. The development of listening can be the basis of initial speaking practice. There should be many opportunities in the class to combine listening and speaking through meaningful activities. Both younger and older learners need plenty of practice with listening and speaking activities and need confidence building to be able to speak up. It is important for teachers to plan both their listening and speaking activities according to their learners' age, interests, and abilities.

Recommended reading

Background theory

Anderson, A. and **T. Lynch.** 1988. *Listening.* Oxford: Oxford University Press.

Bygate, M. 1987. *Speaking.* Oxford: Oxford University Press.

These two books are in the Oxford Language Teaching: a Scheme for Education series. They are comprehensive and very accessible books incorporating the theory of teaching listening and speaking with useful tasks and examples and how to implement them in class. Both these books are an ideal choice for professional development purposes.

Garvie, E. 1990. *Story as a Vehicle.* Clevedon, Avon: Multilingual Matters.

This is a guide for primary teachers offering creative ideas about how to exploit stories for language learning.

Wray, A. 2000. 'Formulaic sequences in second language teaching: principle and practice' *Applied Linguistics* 21/4: 463–490.

This article covers the underlying research and theory of formulaic phrases in speech. It discusses issues of identification and analysis and the significance of formulaic language analysis for practice.

Practical teacher resources

Ellis, G. and **J. Brewster.** 2002. *Tell it Again: The New Storytelling Handbook for Primary Teachers.* London: Longman.

This is an excellent resource for teachers and teacher trainers with some theory and plenty of practical ideas on storytelling. The book is a collection of twelve popular stories used and told all over the world and suggestions to exploit them for learning English as a foreign language.

Martin, C. and **C. Cheater.** 1998. *Let's Join in! Rhymes, Poems and Songs: Young Pathfinder 6.* London: CILT.

This is a practical handbook by CILT aimed at primary foreign language teachers. Even though the activities are for teaching languages other than English, it is still a very useful resource for teachers of English because the discussion and the explanation of the activities are in English. This volume contains some good ideas to introduce songs, rhymes, and poems.

Paran, A. and **E. Watts**. 2003. *Storytelling in ELT.* Whitstable: Kent: IATEFL.

This is a collection of stories used by teachers working with EFL learners all over the world. The book contains the texts of the stories and some recommended teaching tips that worked successfully in classrooms. The book has a substantial section on stories and techniques for young learners.

Satchwell, P. 1997. *Keep Talking: Teaching in the Target Language: Young Pathfinder 4.* London: CILT.

This is another CILT publication for primary foreign language teachers. This volume discusses the advantages of using the target language in the classroom and gives practical tips to put theory into practice.

Wright, A. 1997. *Creating Stories with Children.* Oxford: Oxford University Press.

This is a practical handbook for teachers interested in exploring stories and engaging children in the process of creating their own stories. It contains actual classroom materials with ready-to-use photocopiable sheets.

Tasks

If you would like to look at some practical tasks to explore your own practice related to the content of this chapter, you can try Tasks 2: Observing teachers' language use and 6: Getting children to reflect on their learning (1) (Appendix pages 157 and 159).

6 TEACHING READING AND WRITING

Introduction

Are there any good reasons why reading and writing can be introduced usefully in the TEYL curriculum despite the main emphasis in most programmes on the oral skills of speaking and listening? In order to appreciate the demands of learning to read and write in other languages, this chapter will compare first and second language and suggest ways in which English as a foreign language reading and writing can be introduced and gradually built up with children.

Why teach reading and writing in EYL classes?

Unfortunately there is no formula to follow or no single most effective technique to use when it comes to teaching native speaker children to read English. Needless to say, if there is no formula for teaching reading to children whose first language is English, then there is certainly no formula for teaching reading in English as a second or foreign language because second language contexts can be varied and complex. Whether reading and writing are introduced at all, and if yes, when and how, will depend on many factors such as the age of the children, the level of their exposure to English as a second language, their first language background, and their ability to read in their first language.

In bilingual contexts learning reading and writing in two or more languages often happens at the same time. This means that certain reading skills such as learning to guess the meaning from the context or using illustrations to help with the process of decoding can be transferred between languages. In foreign language contexts, the general consensus is that children should learn to read in their mother tongue first and when they are reasonably competent they can learn to read in a foreign language. It would be controversial to introduce reading and writing in a second language to children who are not yet literate in their first language. However, once literacy in one language is established, children often expect to learn to read in the new language too. In fact, the most convincing reason for teaching reading and writing in English is that many children show both interest and enthusiasm in doing so when they start English. Reading and writing can help to reinforce what they are learning orally. Being able to read or write something meaningful in the second language, such as a party invitation, short message, or shopping list, can give children a real sense of achievement. In addition, exposure to the written record of what is being learnt can be important for those whose learning is more visual and who like to see the words and phrases written down. As children get used to reading and writing in class, these two skills can also open up new opportunities for record keeping. They will also help link children's school learning with their use of English outside class through written homework or reading and writing using the Internet.

Early literacy in English as a first language

In order to make some principled decisions about EFL reading and writing for young learners' programmes, it is useful to explore how children learn to read in English as a first language. The process for EFL learners will be different but this is still a useful starting point because without some familiarity with the process in the first language, the second language process of reading and writing cannot be understood.

Reading and writing during pre-school years

During their pre-school years, English-speaking children learn about literacy in their culture from a range of different experiences. Quite early on, often as early as at the age of three, they begin to recognize written words and signs in their environment such as 'TESCO' or 'PIZZA' or traffic signs. Children who are regularly read to by their parents will notice that story books contain letters and words, in addition to pictures, and that adults actually look at the print to tell the story. Most children also have the chance to observe their parents reading books or newspapers, working on computers, or engaged in other relevant reading and writing activities at home, such as filling in forms and writing lists and cards. All these experiences will prepare children for their own reading and writing. They will begin to see reasons and purposes for reading, such as enjoyment or simply finding out about something, for example, reading the television guide to find out what time a cartoon is on. Children learn very early to write their name and other significant words such as 'mummy' or 'daddy' or a friend's or sibling's name. They will begin to understand that messages, stories, or anything we say can be represented on a page using symbols. By the time children go to school in England at the age of four to five years, they already have a fairly good understanding of many literacy practices and activities and are well on their way to beginning to decode the system of symbols for reading and writing. Building on these initial experiences, the role of the primary school is to carry on with teaching ever more sophisticated literacy skills to children.

Reading and writing at school

Native speaker children possess a great resource to build on when they begin to tackle reading formally at school. This resource is their oral competence in their first language, in particular a large bank of words and phrases. Oral language proficiency is directly related to the ability to learn to read because the solid language knowledge helps children to make intelligent guesses when attempting to read, by simply drawing on what would make sense. This is a great advantage in 'top-down' processing. For example, let us imagine that an English native speaker child is reading the beginning of a story and can work out that the first word is 'Once'. Then without having to read the next word, he can make a reasonable guess that the next phrase is 'upon a time'. This happens because the child knows this phrase is frequently used at the beginning of stories. This knowledge will make it unnecessary to decode the words on the page as if they were in isolation. If there is a meaningful context, the child can make good predictions about what would be a likely phrase or word.

For English-speaking children, the process of learning to read and write takes rather a long time because in English the letter and sound correspondence is not at all direct and consistent. Esther Geva and Min Wang, researchers interested in cross-linguistic perspectives of learning to read, refer in their 2001 survey article to languages such as English as 'deep' orthographies. In English, sounding out the word does not always help with working out how it is written. For example, think of words such as 'enough' and 'thought' or 'height' and 'weight'. The written similarities between these pairs of words do not lead to similar pronunciation. Many other languages that use the Roman alphabet, such as Spanish or German, for example, are called more 'shallow' orthographies because there is more consistency between what a word sounds like and how it is written. In such languages the process of learning to read and write takes less time and appears to be less complicated.

In order to teach aspects of the English system that are regular, English primary schools teach letter–sound correspondence patterns (phonics) to all children. Songs and rhymes are great for teaching phonics because they contain rhyming words such as 'One two three four five, once I caught a fish alive' where 'five' and 'alive' both rhyme and follow the same written pattern. With this approach learners are encouraged to recognize analogies below word level to help them to work out how to read and write words. They are taught to notice that each word has an onset (first consonant or consonants) and a rime (the rest of the word) and it is useful to group words that have a different onset but the same rime because they are pronounced the same way. For example, consider : 'c(at), b(at), m(at), s(at), p(at), h(at), fl(at)'. The initial consonant is salient but the rime of all of these is the same. Recognizing patterns like this will be useful in reading. Traditional nursery rhymes are full of such rhyming pairs, so children find it quite easy to get a feel for rhymes. For example, consider 'the cow jumped over the m(oon)' and 'the dish ran away with the sp(oon)'. Or 'Humpty Dumpty sat on a w(all)' and 'Humpty Dumpty had a great f(all)'. Or 'Jack and J(ill) went up the h(ill)'. Many native English children know these rhymes by heart so it is easy for them to notice the patterns in a meaningful context.

With regard to those words that are irregular, another strategy is used in teaching reading in schools. Often called the whole word method, it encourages the rote learning of some 'sight vocabulary' that children can immediately recognize when reading. This method helps children to see and remember words as visual images. The idea is that these words will be recognized immediately and no further decoding is needed. Knowing a large pool of such vocabulary can help with the initially slow reading speed. Recognizing lots of words is helpful because children can concentrate on processing longer, unfamiliar words.

Teaching reading in EYL classes

In most contexts children do not have a strong background in oral English when they start reading or writing. Their oral proficiency is typically low and they are not necessarily familiar with a wide range of songs, rhymes, and stories in English which carry everyday phrases and words useful for guessing words or for phonics work. Children can only benefit from phonics training if the meaning of the words makes sense to them. It is not good practice to get children to sound out words that they are not familiar with.

However, non-native children also bring some advantages to the process of learning to read and write in English. The greatest of these is their experience with reading in their first language. They usually come to English already able to read and write in their mother tongue and bringing with them some potentially useful strategies. Although the actual first language influences the process of learning to read in English, the point of similarity is that the children have some understanding about what reading is. With regard to the strategies they bring, how they learnt to read in their mother tongue can influence their reading in the second language. They are likely to use strategies that worked in their first language reading, such as spelling, trying to sound things out, comparing sounds and letters. Of course, it is important to remember that the degree to which they have mastered one reading system can vary greatly.

Their first language makes a difference too. There are languages that use morphography or logography, where each symbol represents an idea (such as Chinese, and one writing system of Japanese); or syllabic signs (for example, Korean, where each word is made from alphabet letters which combine into syllables; these in turn combine into a compact character block) and those that use phonography (English, Spanish, or Russian). Naturally, children whose first language uses phonography, and in particular, the Roman alphabet, will find beginning to read and write in English easier than those whose language uses other types of symbols. For example, Russian children learn to read and write using the Cyrillic alphabet, and though this alphabet is closer to English than say Korean or Chinese, it can still present some difficulties. So it will be important to discover the differences and overlaps between the Cyrillic and the Roman alphabets: for example, the children will have to learn that the letter symbol 'P' in English is pronounced as [p] rather than [r] as it would be in their first language. In addition, there are languages that read from right to left and/or bottom to top, and these children will have to start with learning to adapt to a different orientation when using English books.

Reading activities with younger children

As was suggested in the previous chapter on speaking and listening, reading and writing in the primary foreign language classroom do not need to mean fully developed skills from the very beginning. Rather it is advisable to start with working on sub-skills such as learning to decode familiar written language, match spoken and written forms, or complete short texts with personally relevant information. At the beginning of the programme and with younger learners, the teacher might introduce written words to let the children experience printed materials. For example, one could label objects such as tables, chairs, blackboard, window, door, pictures, plants, books, shelves, by making word cards, laminating them, and hanging them up round the classroom. This would make the children curious about reading and writing and could illustrate to them that words that they are familiar with orally can be represented in writing. There are, of course, many other types of writing that can be displayed in any classroom. For example, the teacher can make posters containing commonly used phrases such as 'sit down', 'come here', 'it is your turn', or a calendar with the names of the days and months, or a class birthday chart, or an English noticeboard (see Figure 6.1). All of these visual aids would attract children's attention and help them make the links between spoken and written forms. Teachers can also introduce letter cards or magnetic letters to encourage playing with letters and letter combinations to make words.

Figure 6.1: A classroom full of written language display

Extract 8 (Hicks and Littlejohn 2002b)

Another early activity is to begin to connect spoken words and written words more deliberately by using word cards. Extract 8 was taken from *Primary Colours 1*. This exercise gets the children to practise matching the pictures with the written labels.

In order to practise word level reading, many different games and activities can be used. One well known memory card game is often played by matching pictures and words. Children play in teams picking up two cards each at any one time to see if they match. Similarly games such as 'word snap' or 'dominoes' can be played in small groups or pairs. Teachers can make their own word cards and picture cards and play simple matching or categorizing games or spot the missing card. Many children's coursebooks have their own packs of cards complete with a set of instructions for the teacher. Cards can be used during storytelling as well as other activities for vocabulary teaching. A lot of work with word-cards will contribute to build up children's sight vocabulary of commonly used words in English.

In order to reinforce patterns that are regular in English, it is advisable to include some phonics when teaching children to read and write in a second language. Activities can include categorizing words according to what sounds they begin with and creating sound banks. The difficulty here is that second language learners' knowledge of words to create useful patterns is rather limited at the beginning. With phonics exercises it is important to keep a balance between usefulness and pattern building. If the meanings are unknown, long lists of words exemplifying the same pattern are not useful to children. Familiar songs and rhymes can be exploited in this way to focus children's attention on patterns.

Most beginners' coursebooks also teach the English alphabet, usually in the form of a song. Knowing the names of the letters will not help the children to read but it will enable them to spell words in English. They can practise spelling their own or their friends' names, or play games such as Hangman or simple puzzles such as guessing which letter has been removed from a sentence, or matching letters or dot-to-dot exercises to find words hidden in 'letter boxes'. It is a good idea to display the alphabet in the classroom and practise singing it again and again.

Introducing reading beyond word level should happen gradually. Following on from the practice with word cards, it is of course possible to play with sentences and phrases. The teacher can chop up sentences and get the children to put them back in the correct order. Similarly, familiar songs, rhymes, and poems can also be chopped up and reconstructed. Depending on how familiar the language in these exercises is to the children, the activity can be of varying difficulty. Common sense shows it is best to have plenty of encouraging practice with familiar language first. At a later stage, the teacher can introduce gap-fill activities which combine reading and some writing.

Another supportive way to progress from word reading is to let children follow texts, dialogues, songs, or rhymes in the coursebook while listening to them on the tape. Teachers can get the children to read short texts and dialogues which have been extensively practised orally. This is the case in Extract 9, taken from *Superworld 2*. Children ask each other about their own streets using cut-out buildings and then do a reading activity which is simply matching four sentences of street descriptions with four pictures. The reading is at sentence level. It follows extensive oral practice and is supported by matching visuals.

In the case of younger children it is important to progress slowly with reading in a foreign language. It is a holistic process which involves learning many skills such as predicting, noticing patterns, and guessing. It is a good idea to make this process multisensory by including crafting, colouring, body movements, and sounds. (For more about multisensory teaching see Chapter 1.)

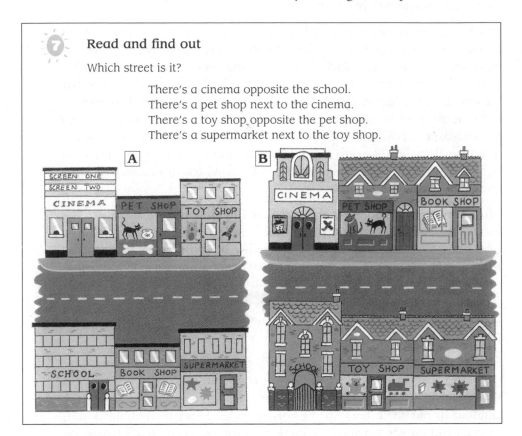

7 Read and find out

Which street is it?

There's a cinema opposite the school.
There's a pet shop next to the cinema.
There's a toy shop opposite the pet shop.
There's a supermarket next to the toy shop.

Extract 9 (Read and Soberon 2000)

Reading activities with older children

The same principle applies here as in previous chapters. Many older children, especially beginners, will enjoy word level and sentence level practice with reading. However, soon they will want to progress further. Reading for meaning entails exercises which encourage children to skim and scan texts in order to understand the meaning. In Extract 10, children have to read the passages and correct sentences underneath. They read for meaning, using their understanding of the passages to work out which statements are true or false.

Extract 10 (Maidment and Roberts 2001)

Older children can be taught that there are many cues that they can use while reading. Semantic cues include those that help them guess the meaning, for example, from illustrations. They will also help as learners look at the structure of sentences and ask questions such as 'Is this a question or a statement?' or 'Is this sentence in the past or in the present?' Phonological cues such as 'how are words like this usually pronounced?' are also useful strategies that can help readers. Older learners often enjoy dictionary work.

They may be introduced to different types of dictionaries such as English–English dictionaries, combined picture and word dictionaries, bilingual dictionaries, or electronic dictionaries. Whatever dictionaries teachers have in the classroom, it is a good idea to begin to use them regularly so that children can develop good dictionary habits such as checking important words and taking notes of synonyms or first language equivalents. In pairs or small groups, children can learn to set each other tasks with dictionaries, such as putting words in alphabetical order or looking up difficult words and letting the other team guess what they mean by choosing the definition that they think is correct.

Teaching writing in EYL classes

What do native speaker children write?

Writing is a complex skill progressing from the level of copying familiar words and phrases to developing an awareness of text structures, genres, the processes of drafting and editing, and writing for an audience. Reading and writing are usually taught in parallel because children who begin to read enjoy writing too. English native speaker children begin with what we call 'emergent writing'. This starts with pretend writing and then gradually they begin to write words and short texts but without knowing exactly how to spell. They incorporate their early phonics knowledge from reading. Emergent writing is often combined with drawings. The example in Figure 6.2 was written by a five-year-old over a period of several months. The progress from pretend writing to simple story writing is very obvious here.

During the first years of formal schooling native speaker children learn tracing and connecting letters to make words. They learn to use basic punctuation marks and start composing passages such as simple story endings and messages, invitations, or cards, slowly progressing towards creative, independent writing and drafting.

Writing activities with younger children in EYL classes

Depending on their specific language background and the type of writing system in their first language, EFL children may need more or less practice with the mechanical basics of writing. It is useful for these children to start with tracing and copying. In order to make these early mechanical activities fun, teachers can vary the activities, for example, introducing creative copying in which children select which words to copy from a list and add one on their own. Other examples may include copying only those words which

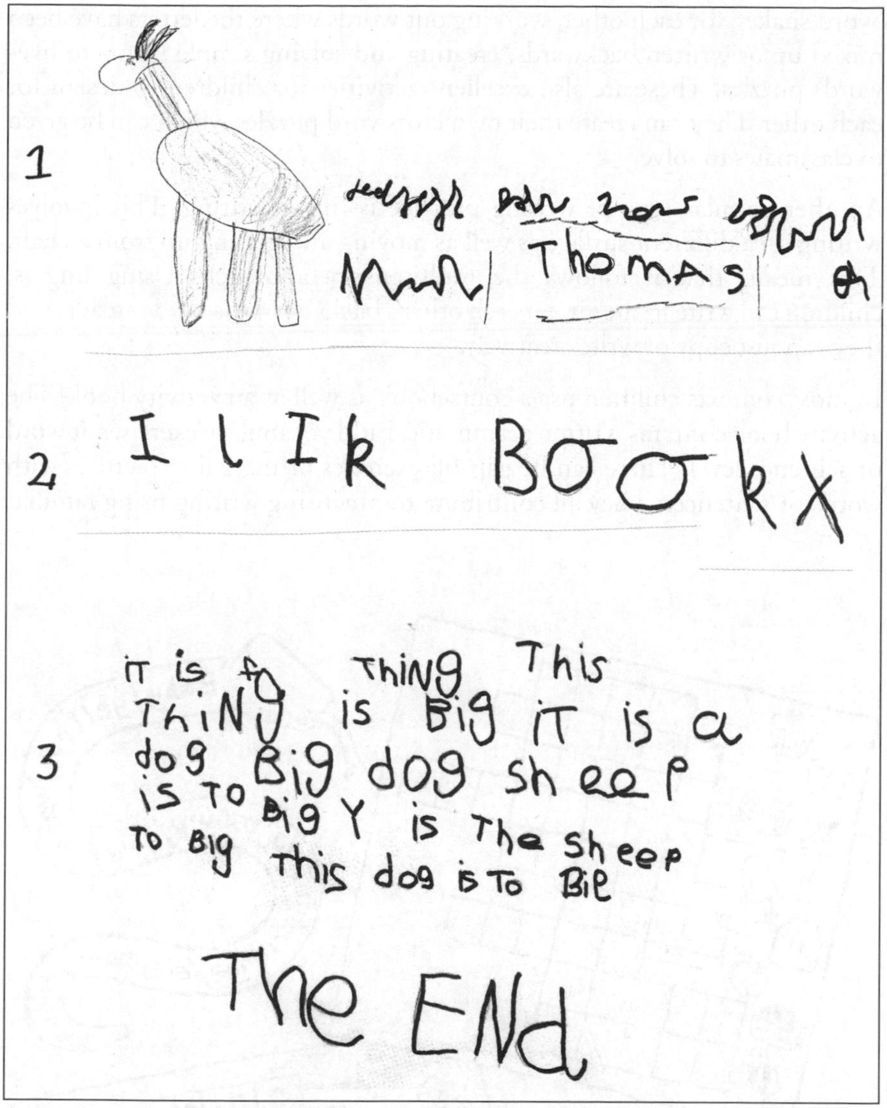

1

edspegl edru znars w8pm
Mrl Thomas *er*

2 I l Ik BoOkX

3 iT is *fg* Thing This
   ThiNg is Big iT is a
   doG Big dog sh ee P
   is To Big Y is The sh ee P
   To Big this dog is To Bie

   The ENd

Figure 6.2: Example of a native speaker 5-year-old's writing

mean some kind of food, or copying only those words which contain the letter T, or copying only those names of animals that appeared in the story. Copying is also done as a follow up to an oral activity. For example, the teacher might get the children to brainstorm lists of words or phrases to write on the blackboard. Later, the teacher can ask the class to copy these words into their exercise books.

Moving on from copying, many games and activities popular in the primary classroom involve word level writing. For example, games such as creating 'word snakes' for each other, working out words where the letters have been mixed up or written backwards, creating and solving simple (four- to five-word) puzzles. These are also excellent activities for children to design for each other. They can create their own crossword puzzles which can be given to classmates to solve.

Another popular type of writing practice is finger writing. This involves writing on a different surface as well as moving and getting up from a chair. This means that it follows the multisensory approach. Using fingers, children can write in the air, on each other's backs or in the sand outside, and they can just copy or write creatively.

In most contexts children use a coursebook as well as an activity book. The activity book contains written grammatical and vocabulary exercises at word or sentence level. These can be gap-fill exercises or matching pictures with words or sentences. They all contribute to practising writing using familiar

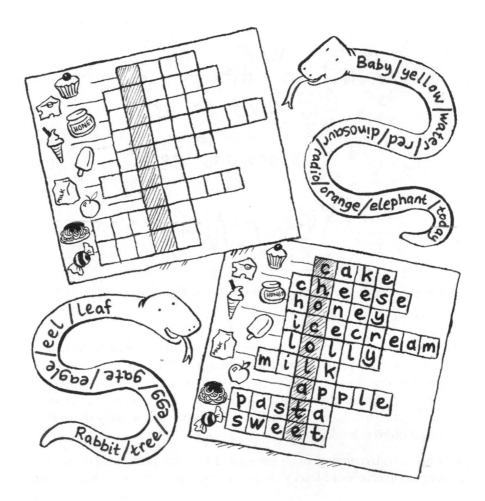

language. Many teachers use guided writing of some kind. This means, just as in guided speaking tasks, that there is a framework or some kind of a model to complete with children's own ideas and relevant details. These are often in the form of cards, invitations, letters, stories, or posters. These genres are important because they can be used to introduce the idea of writing for an audience. Children can begin to see that we write differently depending on who we are writing for. Guided writing activities can be motivating because they allow children to write longer pieces of text by substituting their personally relevant messages into a given frame. These products can also be displayed or taken home. In Extracts 11a and 11b (overleaf), taken from *Jet Primary Resources*, it is very clear that completing such text skeletons can be done at very basic levels, too.

Writing activities with older children in EYL classes

Older learners also need practice with word and sentence level writing and spelling but they may also be ready for freer writing. This can start with filling in captions in speech bubbles in a group cartoon story, or writing instructions, scripts, shopping lists, recipes, puzzles, or simple diaries. The introduction of various written genres will further enhance children's appreciation of different audiences. Older learners may begin to see clear reasons for writing such as to fill in forms, write their own stories, or produce their own class newspaper.

It is good to use word processing because it is possible to have a good quality end product and the correction in editing and redrafting processes is easier and less time-consuming. Computers, of course, are also useful in encouraging written communication with real people such as when a group of children in one country writes to a group of children in another country. Teachers can set up email accounts for everybody in the class and encourage communication within the group both during and after classes. The Internet is a great source of information that children can use with a teacher's guidance. For example, they can search for useful tourist information or timetable details. Creating English websites is a great way of getting older children to practise and enjoy writing. Many good resource books are available to teachers for further ideas.

Children will also use writing for record keeping. Writing lists of new words, dialogues, or short paragraphs in the exercise book is a way of keeping a record of what has been learnt. Teachers can encourage children to evaluate their learning on a regular basis in a personal diary or journal. Initially this is probably best done in the first language but gradually, after mastering some useful phrases (such as 'I enjoyed', 'learnt a lot from', 'did not like', or 'next I would like to learn'), children can begin to reflect on their learning in the second language. (See more about this in Chapter 8.)

Follow-up

1 Pupils can prepare a letter to Santa Claus (see fig 1 below).

Dear Santa Claus
I'd like...........
....
....
for Christmas.
Thank you very much.
From
....

Fig 1

Name .... Class ....

Dear ....

    Thank you for the ....

.... you gave me for Christmas.

.... (It's very

nice/I like it very much/It's just what I wanted).

I am .... (playing

with it/wearing it/looking at it) now.

    I got some other lovely presents too.

My favourite was ....

which I got from ....

It's ....

and ....

    I hope you had a ....

.... (good Christmas/happy

holiday/great festive season).

    Love from

....

Extracts 11a & b (Gray 1996)

Once children can read and write, in many contexts teachers give homework which often involves doing exercises from the workbook. It is worth exploring other fun options for homework such as making puzzles for each other or letting children choose something from a range of tasks. Where teachers are convinced of the positive role of homework in learning, it is important to allocate time to check or discuss this work. Parents who are aware how best to support their children can help a great deal with homework.

Research shows that learners who work together in pairs on tasks that ask them to write texts such as stories or letters do much better together than they could have done on their own. This is because during the process of writing it is important to focus on both the message and the grammatical correctness of the writing. Children can usefully help and scaffold each other during this process. The work of Merrill Swain and her colleagues in Canada (for example, Swain 2000a, Swain and Lapkin 1998) clearly shows that interactive writing tasks can also be fertile ground for learning. Working on a piece of writing together with a friend is also beneficial in terms of sustaining interest and motivation.

Summary

Reading and writing can be useful skills in the TEYL classroom provided that the children are ready and interested in beginning the process of familiarizing themselves with the English writing system. Knowing about reading and writing in English as a first language can be a useful starting point for teachers to make informed decisions about when and how they feel reading and writing should be tackled in their classrooms.

Recommended reading

Background theory

Campbell, R. 2002. *Reading in the Early Years: Handbook.* (2nd edition). Buckingham: Open University Press.

This is an introduction to how native speaker children learn to read in English. It covers many useful topics such as emergent writing, the role of story books and reading schemes, shared reading, whole word approach, and phonics.

Tribble, C. 1996. *Writing.* Oxford: Oxford University Press.
Wallace, C. 1992. *Reading.* Oxford: Oxford University Press.

These two books complete the Oxford Language Teaching: A Scheme for Teacher Education series mentioned in the previous chapter, in terms of covering the language skills. They integrate theory and practice with tasks and materials extracts.

Practical teacher resources

Lewis, G. 2004. *The Internet and Young Learners: Resource Books for Teachers.* Oxford: Oxford University Press.

This resource book is directly aimed at primary English teachers who are interested in exploring the opportunities offered by the Internet in their classes. A range of age groups from eight to 13 is catered for. The tasks are simple to follow and the book contains some useful websites for teachers to explore.

Dudeney, G. 2000. *The Internet and the Language Classroom.* Cambridge: Cambridge University Press.

This is a detailed introduction for teachers to the Internet. It offers some theory and a collection of activities to use with students. Some of them could be easily adapted for primary classrooms. This book also offers advice on the practicalities of creating web pages for classroom use.

Painter, L. 2003. *Homework: Resource Books for Teachers.* Oxford: Oxford University Press.

Although this book is not directly targeted at primary schoolchildren, many of the ideas and the underlying principles can be made relevant for primary English classes. This book encourages teachers to re-examine their homework tasks from a new angle and suggests ways in which homework can be made motivating and encourage learners to continue learning outside the classroom. The author also suggests ways in which homework can be taken full advantage of in the classroom.

Reilly, J. and **V. Reilly.** 2005. *Writing with Children: Resource Books for Teachers.* Oxford: Oxford University Press.

This is a comprehensible collection of ideas about how to introduce and develop writing in primary English classrooms. There are activities which cover the mechanical basics such as tracing and copying and there are also word-, sentence-, and text-level writing exercises. The book emphasizes the idea that writing can be fun and offers opportunities to practise a wide range of writing skills.

Skarbek, C. 1998. *First Steps to Reading and Writing: Young Pathfinder 5.* London: CILT.

This is another volume in the CILT series, other volumes of which have been recommended in previous chapters. This volume discusses ways in which early reading and writing can be successful and motivating in primary foreign language classrooms. The activities are designed for languages other than English but can be equally well exploited in ELT.

Tasks

If you would like to look at some practical tasks to explore your own practice related to the content of this chapter, you can try Task 7: Observing children working together (writing) (Appendix page 159).

7 TEACHING VOCABULARY AND GRAMMAR

Introduction

This chapter looks at teaching the language system, i.e. vocabulary and grammar, to young learners. This discussion overlaps to some extent with ideas and principles from previous chapters. For example, in Chapter 5 there was mention of getting children to listen to songs, rhymes, or stories. These activities aim to practise listening but can also be used to teach new vocabulary and/or grammar. Similarly, in Chapter 6, there were examples of word-level reading and writing games such as matching words with pictures. Such activities can, of course, also be used to practise or recycle vocabulary. Teaching the language skills and the language system are inseparable processes.

Teaching vocabulary and grammar

Vocabulary and grammar are interdependent

Fluent speakers and writers put together the component parts of the language system quickly and efficiently. To be able to do this, they need to know a large pool of vocabulary items and a long list of grammatical structures. However, it is not enough to know these in isolation. Language users also need to understand the complex interaction between vocabulary and grammar. Native speakers put words together quickly in typical combinations and this is what makes them fluent. Such building blocks are often called chunks (see Chapter 5). Speakers store and retrieve phrases such as 'What have you been up to?' as chunks rather than taking each word in isolation. Native speakers also know word collocations, i.e. how words go together naturally, such as 'tall' rather than 'high' to describe trees, or 'take' medicine rather than 'drink' or 'eat'. Vocabulary and grammar are stored together in the mental lexicon in typical combinations rather than in isolation. The implication of this for teaching is that vocabulary and grammar should be taught and learnt together. When teaching vocabulary, teachers may need to consider grammatical choices and environments for the words and when teaching grammar they may need to consider meaningful contexts and typical lexical combinations. When we learn a new word, we have to learn some grammatical information about it. For example, when we learn the verb 'write', we have to learn other related words such as 'a writer', 'a piece of writing', the past tense form 'wrote', and the past participle form 'written'. These words related to 'write' might not all be learnt in primary school but the principles of connecting words to their networks is still important.

From picking up words to knowing words

Vocabulary and grammar are difficult to divide into two distinct areas because lexical choice is always dependent on grammar. When children learn their first chunks of language, these often combine both grammatical patterns and lexis. Younger children, in particular, are not ready for or interested in thinking about the language system or manipulating the language so as to separate lexical items out of structures. They are interested in the meaning and function of new language more holistically, in order to play a game, sing a song, or act out a story. As they grow older, their awareness of language and its component parts grows and the separation and careful analysis of grammar and lexis can begin to take place.

When children pick up new words, they might be able to recognize a vocabulary item without knowing the exact meaning. For example, they might recognize the word 'anteater' in a story or song and infer correctly from illustrations and the accompanying mime that it is some kind of animal. Recognizing 'anteater' in such a context does not mean that children will be able to remember and use the word later in conversation without some deliberate practice and opportunities of use. Children can learn concepts or words in the second language that they do not yet know in their first language. This is natural in a rich linguistic environment.

At a more advanced level, knowing an item of vocabulary will also include being able to spell it correctly and knowing grammatical information about it such as that for example, 'weather' is uncountable as a noun and it collocates with 'nice' rather than 'pretty'. Knowing a word can also be extended to knowing its most common synonyms, such as 'expensive' and 'costly' or 'dear' and antonyms such as 'expensive' and 'cheap'. It is easy to see that the more we know about a word, the more we enter the world of grammar.

Learning grammar is a messy process

All teachers will agree that teaching grammar in isolation, for its own sake, can be a dry and boring activity. It is better if grammar is noticed and learnt from meaning-focused input. This means that grammar emerges from meaningful contexts embedded in appropriate lexis and there is some sort of meaningful communication that leads to focus on grammar. Children need to be able to see the relationship between form and function, what form is used to express what functions and meanings. For example, in the sentence 'Can I have a piece of cake, mummy?' *can* functions as a modal auxiliary of permission, while in the sentence 'Mummy, I can count to 100 in English', *can* is used to express ability. It is important to emphasize that some grammar rules are more consistent than others.

Learning grammar is not a linear process and a lot of intermediate forms are used by learners before they are ready to conform to target language rules. This means that it is natural for children to make mistakes and acquire grammatical forms only partially at first. It is only with continued practice and careful attention that children will finally learn to use correct forms. Children from different language backgrounds go through the same processes and make similar mistakes when learning grammar. This means that the learner's first language is not the only source of errors in second language production. As was suggested in Chapter 2 some mistakes are universal. Learning grammar is a messy process requiring the teacher to provide lots of meaningful practice, recycling, and guidance in attending to language form.

The role of deliberate practice

In both vocabulary and grammar teaching there is a stage when deliberate practice of words or grammatical patterns is used in order to commit the new language to the learners' memory and help them to automatize it so that they can retrieve it quickly and efficiently when needed. Learners will have opportunities to reproduce patterns and vocabulary in a controlled way before expressing their own meanings more freely. Encouraging memorization strategies is an important way to practise new vocabulary. However, it is equally important that learners have the chance to use new language (both vocabulary and grammar) in meaning-focused output in situations where they have control over the choice of language.

Recycling and revising both vocabulary and structures is important in TEYL classrooms. It is essential that recycling remains fun and children do not experience it as a simple repetition of activities from previous classes. For example, board games, class surveys, and project work provide excellent opportunities. Recycling grammar and vocabulary will offer natural opportunities to integrate the language skills.

Vocabulary and grammar for younger children

Learning grammar in a holistic way

For younger children, vocabulary and grammar should be learnt in a holistic way and only when they grow older and begin to show interest in language analysis, can separation begin with the powerful tool of analysis while they continue to learn from rich input. Holistic approaches such as stories are an excellent vehicle to teach vocabulary and grammar together. For example, in the story of the 'Enormous turnip' teachers can revise or teach new vocabulary such as 'turnip', 'old farmer', and 'seed', but these lexical items are learnt in the context of relevant grammatical structures such as the past tense for narrative (for example, The old farmer planted a seed, he looked at it, he couldn't pull it out, a dog walked by, they pulled the turnip out, they cooked some soup, they ate the soup). The past tense will not be analysed or broken into component parts or manipulated in any way but it will be recognized as a natural tense for stories. In this way children will be exposed to the grammar without the pressure of using it. The following example, taken from the resource book *Very Young Learners* by Vanessa Reilly and Sheila Ward (1997), is a good illustration of teaching vocabulary and structure together through a song. Animal names are taught first but also the structure 'It likes (doing something)'. First the children are asked to match pictures of the animals with the words. This is deliberate presentation of the new vocabulary. Then they pretend to be animals, mime the actions, and sing along. No direct attention is paid to grammar. The teacher might tell them the gist of the song in their first language, i.e. what the song is about, if they want to know. The children learn it through active participation, physical actions, and singing along without any reference to first language, manipulation of the component parts, or explanation of the grammar.

Another example that illustrates grammar practice is described by Sarah Phillips' *Young Learners* (1993). The example in Extract 12 practises the structure 'Have you got a (something)?' The teacher prepares two sets of different objects (or cards/pictures) to give out in class. Then the children play a game. Since two of them have the same object, the aim is to find their partners. During the game the children walk around and ask each other: 'Have you got a bike?' or 'Have you got a skipping rope?' The first pair to find their partners are the winners. Whilst at one level this is a grammar exercise, the children enjoy it as a game and take very little notice of the grammatical structure.

Learning vocabulary

Children enjoy vocabulary learning. They pick up new words at an astonishing pace in both their first and second or foreign language and they

5.5 Animals

AGE	**All**
TIME	**5–10 minutes**
AIMS	**Language:** animals, adjectives, *it likes*, action verbs, Total Physical Response **Other:** awareness of animals and their characteristics
DESCRIPTION	The children learn the names of animals, mime them, and sing a song.
MATERIALS	Pictures of wild animals, including: a lion, an elephant, a crocodile, a snake, a monkey, a camel, a hippo, a parrot (see the flashcards on pages 178–82).

IN CLASS

1 Show the children the pictures and tell them the names of the animals. Do this once or twice.

2 Stick the pictures on the board in the order of the song and elicit the names from the children.

3 Ask one of the children to pretend to be a lion. While she/he is doing this, explain that we call the lion 'the King of the Jungle'. (Most children will now be aware of this because of the film *The Lion King*.)

4 Ask another child to pretend to be an elephant. While she/he is doing this describe the elephant's characteristics (big, strong).

5 Continue in this way with the other lines of the song, eliciting the description wherever possible.

6 Sing the song, miming the characteristics as suggested.

7 Sing it again a couple of times, encouraging the children to do the actions and join in.

Animals

The lion is the king of the jungle, / The elephant is big and strong, / The crocodile is very dangerous, / The snake is very long. / The monkey likes to swing through the branches, / The camel likes to walk, walk, walk, / The hippo likes to sit in the mud all day, / The parrot likes to talk, talk, talk, talk, talk. Talk, talk, talk, talk, talk.

The lion is the king of the jungle,	*Walk round looking proud*
The elephant is big and strong,	*Walk round swinging your arm in front of your nose*
The crocodile is very dangerous,	*Open and close your hands like a crocodile's jaws*
The snake is very long.	*Move your arm like a snake*
The monkey likes to swing through the branches,	*Pretend to swing*
The camel likes to walk, walk, walk,	*Walk round*

Extract 12 (Reilly and Ward 1997)

can understand the concept of words well before the concept of grammar. It is a good idea to make deliberate presentation of vocabulary as varied as possible. When presenting vocabulary to the youngest children, teachers can first introduce things they can see, feel, play with, touch, and experience every day. Meaning can be made apparent without the use of the first language. Teachers can use toys, such as dolls to present parts of the body, or puppets to act out a dialogue. They can also use classroom objects such as the desks and chairs, the pictures, and posters. Occasionally, when appropriate, teachers can bring in real objects such as apples, carrots, baskets, bags, hats, bottles, and cups: anything that is easy to pack in a bag or store in the cupboard. Pictures and picture cards are often supplied with young learners' coursebooks together with a set of games and exercises for use. These can also be made at home or teachers can ask children help to make them. Another technique, already mentioned in Chapter 5, is Total Physical Response, which is also used for presenting vocabulary, especially actions and movements (get up, turn around, pick something up). TPR activities will ensure that children can hear the new vocabulary in a meaningful context and respond nonverbally first.

The role of rhythm

Rhyme, repetition, and TPR have been discussed more fully in Chapters 1 and 5. Research shows that in addition to rhyme, mime, and repetition, rhythm also aids vocabulary learning for children. Havovi Kolsawalla, an Indian researcher, demonstrated in a small-scale experimental study in 1999 that rhythmic refrains in stories helped children to remember new language, in particular, new vocabulary. In this study the subjects were five- and six-year-old children who were learning English as an additional language in a British primary school. These children were of course speakers of other languages in their home communities. With the help of the class teacher the researcher divided the children into two comparable mixed ability groups. The researcher selected an ordinary story and rewrote its text in two versions for oral presentation. Since she was interested in the effect of rhythm she rewrote the stories and created rhythmic refrains in the story texts. The rhythmic parts were made up of nonsense words to ensure that the words in focus were genuinely unknown to the children. Rhyming words were avoided to make sure that it was not the rhyme but the rhythm that had the effect. In each version of the story two of the nonsense words were included in the refrain, which was rhythmic, and two in the prose narrative, which was not. The number of times these words were mentioned was also controlled. The stories were narrated to the children twice. All the children in both groups spontaneously recalled the rhythmic elements containing the nonsense words in the refrains but not the nonsense words in the prose narratives. These findings seem to confirm the added benefit of rhythm in vocabulary learning. It is a good idea for teachers to use rich input, i.e. songs, rhymes, rhythmical stories, which captures the natural rhythm of English. Children can move and clap to follow the rhythm.

Incorporating new vocabulary into children's existing knowledge

One important question is just what kind of vocabulary or grammar is suitable in the early years of learning English? Shelagh Rixon, a well known British researcher in the field of teaching English to young learners, in a research article in 1999 examined seven major international children's coursebooks and compared their approach to vocabulary teaching. All seven books were intended for beginning stages of learning for a starting age of about eight years and for a total of about 90 hours of teaching. Interestingly, in terms of the number of words, the books proved to be very different indeed. The amount of vocabulary taught within the given time period ranged from just under 200 items to just under 500 items. There did not seem to be common core vocabulary in that only approximately 50% of all the words appeared in all books. Rixon also found that there was little attention given to working on meaning relationships such as synonyms, subordinates, or categorizing words in useful ways. The majority of words were presented and practised in a static way without the opportunity for the children to see how words interacted with other words in a dynamic way or how the same word can mean different things. For example, if we take a word such as 'chocolate', it can go with adjectives or it can be an adjective itself. It can be used to refer to a drink, a 'hot chocolate', or 'a bar of chocolate', or it can describe a type of cake or ice cream as in 'chocolate cake or chocolate ice cream' (see Figure 7.1). It can even describe a shade of colour as in 'a chocolate brown carpet'. Such richness of meaning was never explored with words in the books that were examined. Vague words such as a 'person', a 'thing', a 'place', or structures such as 'a place where' were not introduced even though they would be very useful for beginner speakers for paraphrasing and explaining. Rixon's conclusion is that teachers may want to find these or other gaps in their textbooks or discover opportunities to seek patterns and notice links between vocabulary items so that lexis can be taught, practised, and recycled in dynamic and meaningful ways. For example, if the children learn the word 'sandwich' in the unit called 'Parties', this is also an excellent opportunity to recycle possible types of fillings the children might know, such as jam, ham, or cucumber sandwich, honey, fish, or cheese sandwich, tomato or chicken sandwich, etc., or even silly ones such as frog or snake sandwiches. As a follow-up, children can invent different sandwiches and put them on the menu of their coffee shop. Activities like this will illustrate to the children that when they learn a new noun such as

Figure 7.1: A semantic network for the word 'sandwich'

'sandwich', it can interact with language they already know. This kind of dynamic view makes vocabulary come alive and paves the path to explicit grammar learning.

Recycling vocabulary and grammar can be a good opportunity to explore words and structures dynamically. For example, children can create 'mind maps' on topics already covered such as 'holidays' or create poster displays with drawings and words. Different board and card games also offer excellent chances to revise and revisit vocabulary or structures. Memory games, such as 'I went to the market and bought …', can be an enjoyable way of revising food or animal vocabulary, but the principle of the same type of memory practice can be extended to other vocabulary such as presents in 'For my birthday I would like …', wild animals: 'In the zoo I saw …', or household objects, such as 'In my cupboard there are …'.

Vocabulary and grammar for older learners

For older learners it is possible to introduce explicit activities which focus on separating vocabulary and grammar. The right time to do this will be when children show an active interest in grammar forms such as by asking the teacher why the verb 'drink' changes to 'drank' but not 'think' to 'thank' in the story or song. Another factor to consider is what grammar the children are learning in their first language. They may be familiar with some metalinguistic terms, that is, terms which allow them to talk about grammar, and which will help them to access similar concepts in English.

Vocabulary activities for older children

With regard to vocabulary, children can continue building their semantic networks mentioned in the previous section. They can also begin to move away from the 'here and now' and learn words that are not visible and touchable, perhaps abstract nouns such as 'friendship' or 'freedom'. Older learners can be encouraged to look up words in dictionaries and begin to interpret dictionary information. They can be introduced to explanations, paraphrasing in the target language, and analytical methods to compare first and second language equivalents, synonyms, and definitions. Recording vocabulary can become more sophisticated and older learners can use a great many useful strategies to help them remember new vocabulary such as practising with cards that have an English word on one side and a synonym or first language equivalent on the other side.

Grammar activities for older children

Language analysis and the introduction of metalanguage can start with simple examples. Extract 13 is taken from Sarah Phillips' resource book *Young Learners*, where children are encouraged to study the component parts of the structure 'Aux + Pronoun + Verb + Noun' as in 'Do you like pizzas?' In the activity the words are jumbled up and the children have to create sentences similar to the model. The activity introduces different colours for the different parts of speech. This gives the teacher the opportunity to teach useful metalanguage. Children can make sentences in groups, pairs, or on their own. As a next step, in order to contextualize this practice, they will make a questionnaire about their eating habits for another class at school or for parents.

Extract 14 is a series of grammar activities for more advanced children. They are taken from a materials project designed by a primary teacher and teacher trainer from Brunei (Shak 2005). This particular series was designed for ten-year-old children who had been learning English for four to five years. The activities practise grammar but also raise children's awareness of grammatical forms in an explicit way by getting them to notice the grammar and talk about it.

The purpose of these activities is to focus on the 'past tense' of both regular and irregular verbs. First of all, the children are invited to look at some text

5.8   Colour parsing

LEVEL	2, 3
AGE GROUP	B, C
TIME	30 minutes
AIMS	**Language:** to learn how a sentence is constructed.
MATERIALS	Coloured chalk, coloured pencils.

PREPARATION

1 Decide which structure you are going to focus on (in this example questions with *like*).

2 Decide on the colours you are going to use. In this case you only need four:

red	*like, love, hate*	(verbs)
blue	*I, you, he, she, etc.*	(subject pronouns)
yellow	*do, does*	(auxiliary verbs)
green	*pizza, coffee, tea, bananas, tomatoes*	(nouns)

IN CLASS

1 Divide your board into two halves. On the left write some words that fit into the sentence structure you have chosen, like this:

```
like  do   you  she
  love   hate  does  he
     coffee  bananas
```

2 Underline the verb in red and invite the children to find and underline other 'red' words. Do the same with the blue, yellow, and green words.

```
like  do   you  she
  love   hate  does  he
     coffee  bananas
```

3 Write your model sentence on the right of the board and ask the children to underline the words in the appropriate colours.

```
like  do   you  she    | Do you like bananas?
  love  hate  does  he  |
     coffee   bananas    |
```

4 Show the children how to make other sentences like yours, using the words on the left. Then they make some of their own, either individually or in groups.

5 Ask the children to tell you their sentences and write them under the model.

FOLLOW-UP

Ask the children to select sentences that would be suitable for a questionnaire about favourite foods.

```
           | Do you like bananas?
           | Does he like pizza?
           | Do you hate bananas?
```

Do the questionnaire (for the technique, see 2.6, 'A questionnaire on health').

COMMENTS

If you are going to use this technique regularly in class, it is worth devising a more complete colour scheme so that you are consistent. Make a poster of it for the classroom wall. Remember that the technique has its limitations and is best used with single structures—if you are not careful the colour coding becomes more complicated than the structure itself!

Extract 13 (Phillips 1993)

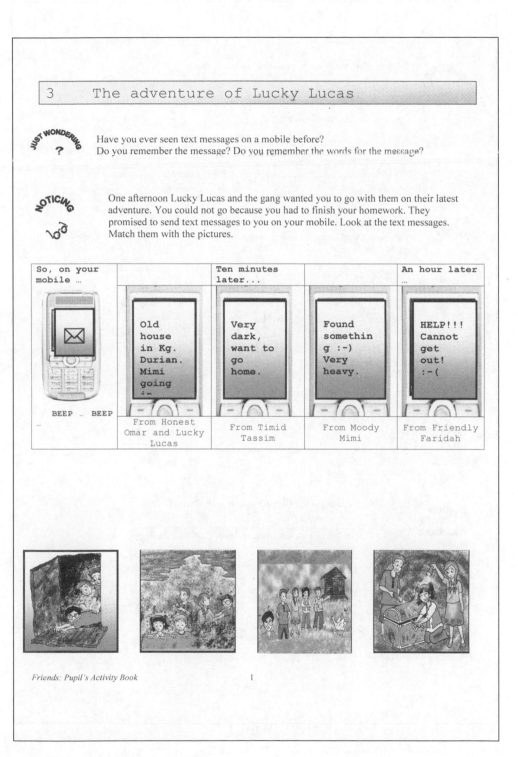

Extract 14 (Shak 2005)

WRITING

Now, complete the story about Lucky Lucas and the gang.

One afternoon Lucky Lucas and the gang _____ an old house in
Kampong Durian. Moody Mimi _____ in first. Timid Tassim
_____ to go into the house because it _____ very
dark. He _____ scared. He _____ to go home. Then
Moody Mimi _____ something. It _____ very heavy.
Friendly Faridah _____ unhappy because they _____

ACTIVITY

Talk to your friend about the story, and check which PAST TENSE VERBS you used in your
story. *Tick the boxes.*

walked ☐	saw ☐	went ☐
ran ☐	did not want ☐	said ☐
found ☐	was ☐	were ☐
climbed ☐	shouted ☐	called ☐
had ☐	fell ☐	came ☐

GRAMMAR DETECTIVE

1. How many PAST TENSE VERBS did you use in your story?

   _____

2. Do you want to make changes to your story?

   _____

YOUR GRAMMAR BOX

Do you want to add anything to your grammar box today?

Remember
:

Extract 14 (Shak 2005)

messages which do not contain past tense verbs and work out what happened in the story by matching the messages to pictures. Then in pairs they try to complete the story using appropriate past tense verbs. As a next step, they are given a list of verbs in the past tense to compare with their solutions and then an opportunity to change their stories. Within the framework of a story, their attention is specifically focused on form and they are invited to reflect on the number of verbs they used. There is a grammar box provided at the end to summarize what they learnt about the past tense in this lesson.

Here is another example which focuses on the use of metalanguage. In this activity the learners focus on editing a letter, in particular the use of punctuation marks. The exercise creates a meaningful opportunity for the learners to talk about the mistakes in the original letters and the corrections in the second version. It is a good idea for teachers to double-check whether the learners know these concepts in their first language yet before doing such an activity.

Fun grammar activities for older learners include puzzles where students are encouraged to discover grammar rules for themselves in games, such as describing differences between two pictures, which can be used to practise prepositions. For learners who also do some writing in English, it is very important to learn about grammar above sentence level. As part of their editing skills, they need to learn about the rules which allow us to link together isolated sentences and paragraphs into coherent texts. Stories and reading passages can be used this way. For example, in Extract 15 from *Tip Top 4*, the text about Boris the Cat, it would be possible to explore the link between the first and the second sentences: 'I've just got a new pet' and 'He is black and white.' The use of the pronoun 'he' indicates that these two sentences are linked together into a coherent piece of text.

Summary

This chapter started out with the idea that grammar and vocabulary were very difficult to divide into two neat categories. Younger learners are simply not ready for and interested in analysing and discussing component parts of the language so vocabulary and grammar are better taught in combination. For older learners it is possible to begin to separate vocabulary and grammar and include more explicit and analytical exercises as well as more use of metalanguage. Recycling is key in both vocabulary and grammar teaching for all children.

(2) **READ, LOOK AND WRITE.**

Mrs Wine is the Editor of the magazine. This means that she chooses the articles, but she also has to correct them before they are printed. She needs to know a lot about punctuation and spelling. Look at the box and find out the meanings of the important words. Then fill in the labels for Susan's article about 'Boris the Second'.

comma [,]   full stop [.]   question mark [?]   exclamation mark [!]

quotation marks [" "]   capital letter [A]   sentence [I've just got a new pet.]

MY CAT,
Boris the Second

I've just got a new pet. He is black and white, and I call him Boris the Second♀. Can you guess why[?]
Well, I enjoyed The [A]dventures of Boris in *Tiptop*, and my new pet is just like him. He is clever and fierce, and he loves eating. I remember that Count Horror found Boris on 29th May⊙ and I found my new cat on the same date! I didn't buy him.
He just came and sat in my garden and asked for food.
He was thin and ill and he had no home, but I looked after him, and now he lives with me, and my family[.]
He is fat and strong now – just like Boris the First[!] We are very happy together.
I hope you like the picture.

Susan from Coventry

1 _____   5 _____
2 _____
3 _____   6 _____
            7 _____
4 _____

Extract 15 (Rixon 1993)

Recommended reading

Background theory

Batstone, R. 1994. *Grammar.* Oxford: Oxford University Press.

This is another volume from the Oxford *Language Teaching: A Scheme for Teacher Education* series. The book explores the nature of grammar and then the teaching of grammar with interesting practical tasks throughout.

Thornbury, S. 1999. *How to Teach Grammar.* London: Longman.

This book explains what grammar is in theoretical terms but it also offers ideas for grammar teaching and sample lessons including a storytelling session with focus on grammar for young learners. It also contains photo-copiable training tasks.

McWilliams, N. 1998. *What's in a Word?: Vocabulary Development in Multilingual Classrooms.* Wiltshire: The Cromwell Press.

This book is for teachers of multilingual classes. It aims to develop teachers' understanding of words and their significance in all areas of the curriculum.

Practical teacher resources

Biriotti, L. 1999. *Grammar is Fun: Young Pathfinder 8.* London: CILT.

This book contains activities and ideas that focus on developing confidence, generating fun and enjoyment with grammar activities in the primary foreign language classroom. One of the aims is to introduce awareness about similarities and differences between languages.

Bourke, K. 1999. *The Grammar Lab: Books 1–2.* Oxford: Oxford University Press.

This is a carefully graded introduction to explicit grammar activities. There are excellent illustrations and imaginative characters making grammar come alive for the children. The activities are mainly games and gap tasks, many to be done in pairs with a friend.

Tasks

If you would like to look at some practical tasks to explore your own practice related to the content of this chapter, you can try Task 8: Exploring textbooks (Appendix page 159).

8 LEARNING TO LEARN

Introduction

'Learning to learn' is one of the most important objectives for all learning/teaching contexts for all ages. In our fast moving world, it is simply impossible for learners to acquire all the knowledge and skills they need while they are at school. It is the school's responsibility to teach learners how to learn, i.e. to equip them with strategies that they can use outside school. This process needs to start as early as possible, preferably at the beginning of schooling. Various aspects of 'learning to learn' can be introduced into the day-to-day practice of any language classroom without changing many of the usual classroom practices. This chapter will discuss explicitly some opportunities that teachers of English for young learners can take to promote principles of 'learning to learn'. Most of the suggested techniques and ideas can be adapted to all types of contexts and can work in large classes as well as mixed ability classes.

What is 'learning to learn'?

The overall aim of incorporating some kind of 'learning to learn' is to begin to raise children's awareness of the various factors that influence their language learning and to give them some time and space to start to think for themselves. 'Learning to learn' is a broad concept which can encompass a great variety of different activities, tasks, or discussions between children and the teacher. Some teachers might be working in contexts where 'learning to learn' is explicitly incorporated into the curriculum guidelines and both the national curriculum and the recommended coursebook contain specific advice on the techniques and activities used and the rationale behind them. Others might not have such explicit guidelines to work from but would be free to use their own ideas.

In this chapter 'learning to learn' activities are divided into three main categories. This list offers some ideas to begin to explore learning to learn, but is by no means complete. Teachers are invited to add/adapt as they see fit.

What types of strategies can be developed?

1 **Social and affective strategies**: to raise awareness about how learners' own emotional states and feelings as well as those of others can influence their learning. Activities in the classroom can include teacher-led discussions, usually in the mother tongue, about the social aspects of learning, such as the importance of listening to each other, turn taking in games, or controlling shyness and fear of speaking out in front of others. As part of developing awareness about affective factors, teachers can give plenty of praise and positive feedback to children to raise their self-esteem and self-confidence as well as boost their motivation.

2 **Strategies related to raising awareness about what language learning is**: to cover general understanding about language learning. In terms of understanding what language learning means, teachers might discuss with children how long it takes to learn a language, why it is important to practise, or why we all make mistakes.

3 **Metacognitive strategies**: to introduce and develop the ongoing process of reflection through planning, monitoring, and evaluating language learning. Activities in the classroom can include encouraging children to think about what they did well and why, and what they enjoyed and why. At later stages, children can be prompted to think about the reasons for doing various activities and tasks and about lessons that can be learnt from each learning experience.

4 **Direct or cognitive strategies**: to develop children's ability to deal with linguistic information in an effective way, i.e. to organize, categorize, or memorize linguistic information. Activities in the classroom can include training strategies such as how to remember a list of words, how to guess the meaning of unknown words in a text, or how to link unrelated language to aid memory.

The above categories have been listed to illustrate an order in which they can be introduced. Teachers can start with emotions, feelings, and boosting self-esteem. They can then introduce metacognitive strategies which can be made applicable to any unit of learning. Finally, the cognitive strategies with older or more experienced learners can be added. This of course does not mean that this order must always be followed. Teachers are encouraged to judge for themselves what is appropriate and feasible. Some schools may be fostering learning to learn strategies in the other areas of the curriculum, which gives teachers a good chance to integrate English into an existing framework.

Developing social and affective strategies and raising awareness about language learning

Activities for younger children

This aspect of 'learning to learn' can be the foundation for all children. In terms of the affective factors, all teachers of children are concerned with issues such as building confidence and raising self-esteem. Without these and a positive learning environment full of encouragement, it is impossible to achieve the goals related to fostering positive attitudes. The younger the children are, the more important these considerations become. The teacher can be an important role model, displaying positive, cheerful behaviour and friendliness at all times. This is particularly important because younger children see the teacher as a source of motivation. (See more about this in Chapter 4.) All teachers can foster children's self-esteem by emphasizing what children can do rather than what they can't do. Asking children's opinions about the English lessons and their own progress are fundamental parts of building self-reliance and awareness. Gaining experience in expressing their opinions is a good foundation for self-assessment. (There is more about self-assessment in Chapter 10.) Children's simple reflection notes about their progress should focus on what has been achieved rather than where the gaps are. Evaluation sheets should always be phrased in a positive way such as:

- I can sing a song.
- I can tell a story.
- I can talk about my family/friend.
- I can write a postcard.
- I can . . .

Teachers should provide positive reinforcement, and use plenty of praise when commenting on children's work and performance in English. They can also show their appreciation by displaying children's work on the wall or by giving feedback to individuals. It is important for teachers to encourage children to express their feelings and to listen to those who have something important to say before the lesson begins. Young children are often much more affected by events at home than older ones. Teachers of very young children might find it useful to listen to children talking about falls, lost pets, or the birth of a baby brother or sister. The fact that the teacher knows about their concerns will give young children a sense of security.

In terms of social development, it is important for teachers to be sensitive to individuals and friendship groupings. They may want to promote co-operation, listening, and turn taking in order to train children specifically in developing skills of working effectively in pairs or groups. Children need to begin to understand that different people see things differently and it is important to be tolerant of others. Drawing up class rules together is an effective way to start establishing what is acceptable during English classes. Children should be involved in this process so that they can feel they have some control over what is happening.

With regard to the nature of language learning it may be appropriate, for example, to talk about general expectations in learning languages. How much can we learn in a week, a month, or a year? What will we be able to do in English by the end of the school year? These discussions can happen in the mother tongue and do not need to take up a lot of time, perhaps just five to ten minutes a week. However, once they are introduced, it is a good idea to incorporate them regularly. Teachers can share anecdotes and interesting facts about language learning. Many children will be fascinated by this and will have their own insights to offer.

Activities for older children

For older learners, rather than just focusing on the English language, it is also possible to raise awareness about other languages, how languages are different, or how many languages are spoken in the world. Such an extension of their understanding about languages and language learning can feed into other areas of the curriculum such as geography or history. For example, in Extract 16, from *Story Magic 3*, children learn about where different languages are spoken and make discoveries about the world they live in. This particular unit is concerned with English, Spanish, and Arabic but of course the teacher can use other languages including the children's own mother tongue. This can be followed by a quiz or a survey of who speaks what languages in the school or in the community.

With older groups teachers can develop children's skills in working col-laboratively, or they can consider affective factors in some detail, or encourage children to continue their discoveries about language learning, for example, through the comparison of their mother tongue with English. Regular discussions can help children to become more aware of what is involved in language learning as well as help them cope with ups and downs, or days when they find it a bit less exciting. Such self-motivation was discussed in Chapter 4, too. With older learners teachers can include discussions about the need to practise regularly, and the need to be patient when you are learning a new language.

Fact file

Traveller's guide

Languages

They speak English in 45 countries.
They speak Spanish in 22 countries.
They speak Arabic in 19 countries.

Mountains

The Atlas Mountains are in Morocco.
The Picos de Europa are in Spain.
The Rocky Mountains are in the USA.
The Blue Mountains are in Australia.

Capitals

The capital of the UK is London.
The capital of Spain is Madrid.
The capital of Morocco is Rabat.
The capital of Peru is Lima.
The capital of Australia is Canberra.

Rivers

The Ebro is in Spain.
The Nile is in Egypt.
The Mississippi is in the USA.
The Thames is in the UK.
The Darling is in Australia.

8 Read and answer the questions.

1. What is the capital of the UK?
2. Where is Canberra?
3. Where are the Atlas Mountains?
4. Name a river in Egypt.
5. They speak English in 22 countries. True or false?

Project

9 Make a country poster.

Morocco

This is Morocco. The capital city of Morocco is Rabat. They speak Arabic in Morocco. The Atlas Mountains are in Morocco.

10

Extract 16 (House and Scott 2003b)

Developing metacognitive strategies

Learning to reflect

Learning a foreign language at school means being actively involved in a range of different activities such as listening to a story or the teacher talking, answering questions, creating dialogues with a friend, or writing a short paragraph. It is important that children begin to understand why these activities are used in the classroom and how they can participate effectively. Such reflection on the learning process is a natural part of effective learning and can be adapted at the level of individual activities, tasks, lessons, or even larger units such as terms and school years. In other words, learners can reflect about how well and why they answered a question and why or how well they did with the dialogue or role-play. In the latter example, it would be possible to think about whether each speaker contributed fully, whether they listened to each other, whether they rehearsed effectively, or whether they managed to control their nervousness in front of the class. Reflection is also important when teachers and learners take stock of what has been achieved at the end of a school term or year. Developing metacognitive awareness is, of course, directly linked to developing self-assessment, which will be discussed in the next chapter.

Explicit reflection is often fostered in coursebooks for children. Extract 17 is taken from *New English Parade 6*, which uses regular activities to encourage reflection about what has been learnt by introducing the 'journal'. The journal simply refers to a section of the pupils' book which prompts the children to complete the sentence which begins: 'Now that I have completed this unit, I can …'.

This particular example is in English but such reflections can also be carried out in the mother tongue, if more appropriate.

Activities for younger children

For the youngest age group, this reflection process may start by asking children to think and decide which activities they liked in a lesson or a unit. At the end of a lesson the teachers can simply ask children to put their hands up to show the activities they enjoyed most. Simple but creative illustrations (for example, 'smiley faces' or 'rabbit ears', where the position of the ears, up or down, means good or bad) can be used to represent categories such as 'I like it very much', 'I'm not sure' or 'I don't like it'. Extract 18 shows an example of an evaluation sheet.

Once they can identify their favourite activities, it is useful for children to begin to think about reasons. These simple activities will encourage them to pause and think for themselves and come up with reasons why they like or dislike certain tasks. If such reflection is carried out on a systematic basis, the children will get used to having to think for themselves and the teacher will gain insights into their motives and developing opinions.

The above examples are restricted to reflecting about a learning experience after it has happened. However, the 'plan–do–review' reflective cycle can be extended to thinking ahead before doing an activity, or thinking while doing the activity, not just thinking about how it went and why. This three-step process is often referred to as the 'metacognitive' cycle (see Figure 8.1).

> **My Journal**
>
> 1. My earliest memory is when I _____
>   _____.
>
> 2. Words that describe me are _____, _____
>   and _____.
>
> 3. One thing I haven't done that I want to do is to _____
>   _____.
>
> 4. Now that I have completed this unit, I can _____
>   _____.

Extract 17 (Herrera and Zanatta 2001b)

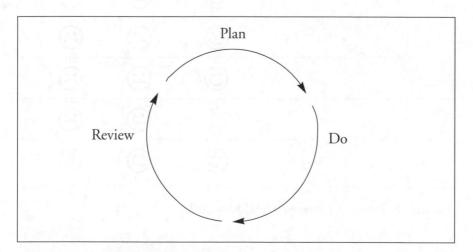

Figure 8.1: 'Plan–do–review' cycle

How I like to learn English

Name: _____ Class: _____ Term: _____			
I like:	☺	😐	☹
learning English	☺	😐	☹
my books	☺	😐	☹
watching videos	☺	😐	☹
listening to cassettes	☺	😐	☹
singing songs	☺	😐	☹
role play	☺	😐	☹
playing games	☺	😐	☹
learning about other people	☺	😐	☹
reading stories	☺	😐	☹
	☺	😐	☹
	☺	😐	☹
	☺	😐	☹
	☺	😐	☹
	☺	😐	☹

Extract 18 (Ioannou-Georgiou and Pavlou 2003)

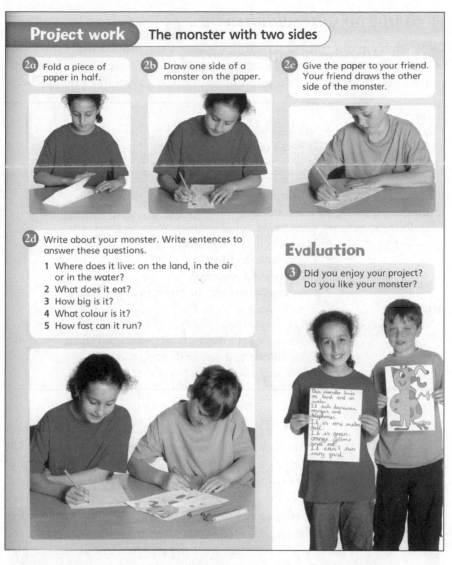

Extract 19 (Hicks and Littlejohn 2003)

It is possible to introduce a general methodology for developing a 'plan–do–review' cycle in most learning situations.

Some primary coursebooks incorporate aspects of the metacognitive cycle. For example, in Extract 19, taken from *Primary Colours 3*, pairs of children make monsters and then write about them following a set of questions in the book. At the end of the activity they are encouraged to think about the process and say whether they enjoyed participating in the project, and whether they liked their monsters. At this simple level it can probably be done in the second language, which is what the coursebook suggests.

Activities for older children

Older children can think more explicitly about the process using questions at each stage of the activity. When a group of children are planning a mini-project they may consider the questions in Table 8.1, with the teacher's help:

Before:
Planning stage
- What do we have to do here?
- Have we done this before?
- How can we build on what we already know?
- How many ideas have we got to start with?
- Which shall we do first?

During:
Monitoring stage
- How are we doing so far?
- Have we got enough time?
- Do we have to change our plan?
- Have we got a problem?
- How can we sort out the problem or get help?

After:
Evaluating stage
- What did we learn?
- What did we enjoy about this project and why?
- What did we find easy or difficult and why?
- How can we do it better next time?

Table 8.1: The metacognitive cycle

One helpful way to foster metacognitive growth is to encourage explicit analysis of tasks and games in order to learn to play them better. The teacher can talk children through how to play a game. This is a kind of 'scaffolding' referred to in Chapter 1. For example, let us imagine that a teacher wants a group of ten-year-olds to play a guessing game in which they ask questions to guess what the teacher has got in a 'magic box'. Before starting the game, the teacher might want to think together with the children about how to play the game. What types of questions would help them to succeed? For example, considering the size of the box or the bag, certain objects would be excluded. It is useful to think: what sort of things are of that size? It is also important to listen to other people's questions and the teacher's answers in order to put all useful information together. It is necessary to double-check if something was not understood because if children miss some important clues, they have no chance of guessing the object.

For older groups it might be possible to start recording learning by building up a 'learning tree' or a 'learning wall' at the back of the classroom (see Figure 8.2). At the end of every week the teacher can ask the children to think about what they learnt that week. Then the ideas/suggestions can be put up on to the tree as leaves. Depending on the children's ability to read, it is possible to use drawings instead of writing on the leaves. The tree will grow more and more leaves as the weeks go by and the children will have an explicit record of what they have done. The leaves can be moved around to show how learning different things can link to previous knowledge.

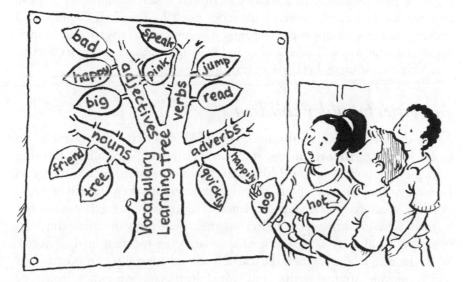

Figure 8.2: A learning tree

Developing cognitive strategies

Language learning often requires manipulating linguistic information in an effective way. There are specific strategies to help language learners such as organizing, rehearsing, using different visual and other meaningful clues, predicting, and using deduction while listening or reading. These are often referred to as direct or cognitive strategies. For example, children will have to memorize and categorize words, learn rhymes by heart, or predict information while listening to a story. Teachers can help them to learn effective ways of doing these.

Activities for younger children

For the youngest age groups teachers may start developing cognitive strategies slowly and carefully. For example, in classes where children often perform short dialogues in front of their friends, teachers might want to begin to encourage rehearsal strategies. Children can be given explicit advice as to how to help each other and what clues they can use to remind themselves of what comes next. Another early strategy is the development of predicting skills during storytelling sessions. Teachers can start by simply asking the children to say what they think will happen next. Carried out systematically this training will help them to make predictions in other situations as well. It is also a good idea for children to have their own English picture vocabulary books. They can begin to explore ways in which they can organize new language. In Extract 20, from *Primary Colours Starter*, the children are invited to make an alphabet book by drawing, cutting, and sticking pictures on appropriate pages. The process of organizing known vocabulary this way will aid learning and will offer an example of an effective categorization strategy in language learning.

Activities for older children

At the other end of the continuum, with older children it is possible to do more sophisticated organizing and categorizing of vocabulary learning strategies. Hanne Thomsen (2003), a classroom practitioner working in Denmark, has written about training children in their fourth year to develop vocabulary learning strategies. Throughout several lessons her learners were encouraged to reflect on their own ways of organizing and recording vocabulary as well as their own strategies for memorizing words. With the help of the teacher, the learners started compiling on posters lists which include strategies that individual learners used either inside or outside the classroom. All the strategies were discussed as they were added to a poster and good strategies were highlighted. For example, one learner suggested recording new vocabulary in a book together with synonyms and example sentences. Learners were encouraged to choose a vocabulary recording system to suit their taste but good models were discussed and shared by everyone. Such discussions can be very useful in children's first language too, if their language level does not permit them to be in English.

Giving space to children's choices

In order for children to be able to put their developing strategies into practice, it is a good idea to give them more space and time during lessons. This means that teachers will have to let go of their total control of the classroom and involve children in the decision making process. Allowing children to make some choices and initiate ideas during English lessons is motivating for them because this will lead to more active involvement and more enjoyable learning. Listening to children's voices also sends out the clear message that their interests and opinions are valued and appreciated by the teacher.

It is of course important to offer only limited choices at the beginning. For example, for the youngest groups, when teachers introduce vocabulary such

Extract 20 (Hicks and Littlejohn 2002a)

as 'wild animals' it is a good idea to let children brainstorm in the mother tongue names of animals that they want to learn rather than present them with a predetermined list. They may have their own favourite animals. It is possible to prepare two or three similar tasks and give children a choice of which animal they want to read or write about. Even if there is hardly any difference between these texts and tasks from the teacher's perspective, the children will experience it as a real choice.

There are many other ways in which teachers can encourage children's involvement through recognizing and respecting their choices. They can try to set freer homework tasks. For example, children can learn three new vocabulary items of their own choice every week on top of what is learnt by everybody. They can look words up in a picture dictionary, ask their older siblings for ideas, or choose words or phrases from their favourite comics or books or even the Internet. In class they can make displays of their words and/or keep a personal vocabulary book. What matters is that their own involvement in choosing these words will make the language more relevant to them and this will increase the likelihood of remembering and learning. At the beginning of the next lesson children can be put into small groups to tell each other what new words they learnt.

Another small step towards giving children choices is to start a modest self-access corner in the classroom with activities and exercises organized systematically in a cupboard or a box. For a start there could be some crossword puzzles in the corner, and later on teachers can add some picture books and then maybe games to be played in teams or pairs. It is possible to allow just fifteen minutes each week when children can choose something from the corner to look at and work with individually or in small groups. It is possible to build this up gradually and change the tasks and activities as needed. Children can help build it up by creating tasks and activities for each other such as word snakes, crossword puzzles, or other tasks. Teachers may find it very beneficial to collaborate with others to pool their resources.

Offering choices to children and encouraging their independence in small ways is also consistent with the principle advocated in this book that all children's needs are different and it is important for teachers in language classes to cater for individual learner differences, interests, and needs. For example, a motivated high achiever will find it exciting to be able to rise to the challenge of his or her own choice. Equally, learners who are progressing more slowly might need the time to consolidate something quietly while the others are engaged with more demanding tasks.

Raising awareness about the learning process, developing language learning strategies, and giving children some freedom in their learning, are all principles which, taken together, can foster independent learning in classrooms. This means systematic awareness raising, preparing children for future learning and encouraging a reflective attitude to learning without much change to the usual content and procedures.

Summary

In young learners' classes, there will of course be great differences between what is possible to achieve in different age groups. The younger the learners, the less they are able to stand back and reflect on their own learning, or choose for themselves, plan, or evaluate their performance. However, even the youngest children will be able to respond well to small steps taken in the direction of 'learning to learn'. Incorporating some 'learning to learn' activities into language learning is beneficial both for the children and the teacher. The children gradually learn useful skills that can be applied to other areas of learning and become more aware and self-confident, and the teachers can discover more about their learners.

Recommended reading

Background theory

Dam, L. 1995. *Learner Autonomy 3: From Theory to Classroom Practice.* Dublin: Authentik.

Based on many years of work as a classroom teacher, Dam explains what learner independence means in her classrooms, what the teachers' and the learners' roles are, what sorts of problems occur in these classrooms, and what the benefits are.

Practical teacher resources

Chambers, G. and **D. Sugden.** 1994. 'Autonomous learning—the Danes vote yes!' *Language Learning Journal* 10: 48–57.

This article is a lively description of what happens in some Danish primary classrooms where learning to learn principles are systematically applied.

Datta, M. and **C. Pomphrey.** 2004. *A World of Languages: Developing Children's Love of Languages: Young Pathfinder 2.* London: CILT.

This is another CILT volume in the series for primary language teachers. This volume aims to celebrate linguistic variety in multilingual contexts. Some activities focus on formal aspects of language but the main aim is to foster curiosity and confidence among young language speakers.

Phillips, D., S. Burwood, and **H. Dunford.** 1999. *Projects with Young Learners.* (Resource Books for Teachers). Oxford: Oxford University Press.

This book offers good ideas for planning, organizing, and implementing project work with children. The activities cover all skills and a wide variety of topic areas. Project work encourages children to make choices and decisions for themselves and eventually to learn to work more independently.

Tasks

If you would like to look at some practical tasks to explore your own practice related to the content of this chapter, you can try Tasks 9: Observing children working together (speaking), 10: Observing children choosing tasks, and 11: Getting children to reflect on their learning (2) (Appendix pages 159 and 160).

9 MATERIALS EVALUATION AND MATERIALS DESIGN

Introduction

The most important teaching and learning material that guides teachers' and learners' activities in many classrooms seems to be the coursebook. Modern coursebooks come with useful accessories such as a teacher's resource book or resource pack, an activity book for students, tapes, CDs, word and picture cards, posters, and photocopiable materials. Young learners' coursebooks are well designed with attractive features such as colourful visuals, fun games and tasks, crafts, and projects, yet it is important to note that no coursebook can be perfect for any teaching and learning situation and this is why teachers find materials evaluation and materials design very useful skills. This chapter will take teachers through the steps of evaluating and supplementing coursebooks and creating their own materials.

Using coursebooks

In some contexts teachers follow a set coursebook very closely lesson by lesson and exercise by exercise, while in others teachers are able to select their own materials and activities more freely. Realistically, most teachers are somewhere in the middle, where there is a coursebook to follow but there is also some scope for individual contributions. Most countries have national syllabus guidelines and objectives for primary English. Ministries of Education often identify a list of recommended books that schools can choose from. Since many international young learners' coursebooks cannot meet special local expectations or needs, individual countries develop their own textbooks.

Multilayered syllabuses

Most modern primary coursebooks follow what we call a 'multilayered' syllabus which means that in addition to the traditional structural and functional language components, other components such as topics or

Aims	Main language children use	Main vocabulary	Main receptive language
Introduction Hello, Max!			
To introduce yourself To state and ask age To identify colours	*What's your name?* *I'm (Eddie).* *Hello. Goodbye.* *How old are you?* *I'm (7).* *What colour is it?* *It's (red).*	Numbers 1–10 red, yellow, green, blue, pink, purple, orange, black, brown, white, grey	*Open your (Pupil's Book) at page (1).* *Now look at (Activity 2) on page (2).* *Find (the word).* *Pupil's Book* *Activity Book* *Let's (play a game)!* *cassette, magic wand, coat, star, number*
Unit 1 Max's magic book			
To identify and ask about classroom objects To talk about possessions To describe the colour of classroom objects	*What's this?* *What's in your school bag?* *It's (a pencil case).* *my, your* *Is this your (ruler)?* *Yes, it is. No, it isn't.* *What colour's your (pen)?* *It's (green).*	book, pencil case, school bag, pen, ruler, pencil, rubber	*Hold up (your book).* *Show me (Max).* *Open/Close (your eyes).* *Listen to (the words).* *Ready for school?* *Well, put it in your bag!* *Come on! It's time to play!* *What's missing?* *What a mess!* *Count the (pencils).* *magic book*
Unit 2 A house for the animals			
To identify animals To describe animals using adjectives	*What's that?* *It is (a tiger). It's (a dog).* *It isn't (a cat).* *Is it (a mouse)?* *Is it (small)?* *A (giraffe) is (tall).* *An (elephant) isn't (small).*	tiger, crocodile, wolf, dog, cat, monkey, lizard, elephant, mouse, giraffe big, small, tall, fat, dangerous	*Point to (the tiger).* *This is (Nick).* *Can you see (the animals)?* *Who's that?* *Now complete (the sentences).* *Choose (a colour).* *True or false.* *jungle, house, mammals,* *reptiles, Out!* *The (wolf) is too (big).*
Unit 3 Lucy at school			
To identify school rooms and furniture To state and ask about the location of objects To describe a picture	*Where's the (blue fairy)?* *In the (library).* *Where are you?* *I'm in the (gym).* *Is the fairy (under)* *the (chair)?* *There's (a cat on* *the table).* *There are (three books* *on the shelf).*	classroom, library, gym, playground, park, toilets in, on, under table, chair, shelf, cupboard right, left	*Put the pictures in order.* *school, fairies, school report, then* *Is there a fairy in the (library)?* *Run, Lucy, run!* *Red light. Stop!* *Green light. Go!* *Look right and left.* *Cross the road.* *Be careful!*
Unit 4 The snowman's scarf			
To describe clothes and what people are wearing To ask and describe what the weather is like	*Put on your (coat).* *What is (Alice) wearing?* *I'm/He's/She's wearing* *(green gloves).* *He/She isn't wearing* *(a blue hat).* *What's the weather like today?* *It's (hot). It's (raining).*	jumper, skirt, trousers, T-shirt, socks, shoes, coat, hat, gloves, boots, scarf cold, hot, sunny, windy, raining, snowing	*Tell your friend.* *Draw a (picture).* *Fold the paper.* *snowman, footprints, lonely,* *boy, girl, friend, message,* *grandma* *What's the matter?* *Don't worry!*

Extract 21 (House and Scott 2003a)

themes, phonology, cultural components, or learning to learn skills, are
included. Extract 21 is from *Story Magic 1*, a publication by Macmillan.
Whilst it is true that there are many components in a multilayered syllabus,
there is one primary component that drives the process of planning. This is
often referred to as the 'main organizing principle'. In this outline the main
organizing principle is the series of topics identified on the left-hand side of
the syllabus outline (such as 'Max's magic box', 'A house for the animals',

Main recycled language	Sounds	Skills * Skills marked with an asterisk are repeated in every unit	Attitudes	Cross-curricular theme	Multi-disciplinary link
		Showing understanding through a song.* Following oral and written instructions.* Asking and responding to questions.* Using a key to colour in a picture. Following instructions to make a cut-out magic wand.	Showing an interest in starting to learn English. Participating in a song with actions and mime. Realizing the value of using English in class.	Good citizenship: learning how to introduce yourself in English	Music and dance: singing a song with actions and mime
Numbers 1–10 Colours What colour is it? It's (blue).	/ə/ /iː/	Matching words and pictures.* Listening to a story.* Showing understanding by re-ordering events in a story.* Reading and joining in with a story.* Listening to and identifying different sounds.* Creating a poster.* Reading for pleasure.* Acting out a story.* Compiling a picture dictionary.*	Showing an interest in communicating in English. Enjoying listening to and joining in with stories. Participating in activities with others in class.	Moral education: tidying up	Maths: counting objects and completing a pie diagram
Colours What colour is it? It's (green). What's this?	/l/ /aɪ/	Completing a crossword. Using judgement to make decisions. Choosing the correct word following visual prompts. Categorizing vocabulary. Saying a chant with actions and mime. Completing a chart. Following instructions to make a cut-out snapdragon. Listening for information.	Showing an interest in wild animals. Willingness to do the task properly. Co-operating in group and pair work.	The environment: learning about where animals live	Environmental studies: classifying animals into reptiles and mammals
Numbers 1–10 Colours What colour is it? It's (yellow).	/ʌ/ /uː/	Playing a game to practise key vocabulary. Identifying the correct written information. Listening to match words and pictures. Saying a spell with key vocabulary. Using cut-out materials to play a game. Saying a rhyme with actions and mime. Matching sentences and pictures.	Showing an interest in school. Using English to play communicative games. Turn-taking and respect for others.	Road safety: crossing the road safely	Geography: identifying location and direction using left and right
Colours He/She is (big). He/She isn't (a snowman). It's ...	/ɒ/ /əʊ/	Giving and following oral instructions. Colouring a picture following oral prompts. Writing missing information. Using cut-out materials to play a game and complete sentences. Saying a chant with actions and mime. Drawing and describing a picture. Responding to written questions.	Joining in with a group dance. Participating in a game and respecting the rules. Working together to complete activities.	Health education: wearing the right clothes for the weather	Environmental studies: * identifying different weather conditions

'Lucy at school'). Indeed a great many coursebooks are topic-based because topics fit well with holistic learning. Each of the topics in this book generates language naturally through the stories, games, and tasks. For example, in Unit 3, under the topic heading 'Lucy at school' we can see listed the structures 'there is/there are' and school-related vocabulary such as *library, playground*. The vertical columns in the outline correspond to the other 'layers'. There is a column for main language structures and vocabulary that the children will use in activities but there is also a column for receptive language. By receptive language, the designers mean that children will hear this language, for example, in storytelling, but will not have to use or manipulate it in any way. This is consistent with the principle mentioned in Chapter 5 that it is good for children to be exposed to rich language through input. A separate column has been devoted to recycling language in the syllabus to show that this aspect of the course is systematically planned and recycling occurs in every unit. There is also additional focus on specific sounds and skills. Beyond the linguistic criteria there are three more columns: one is for developing positive attitudes, specifically here positive attitudes to school; one is for introducing links with other areas of the curriculum, in this unit road safety. The final column is for developing multidisciplinary links, for example, reinforcing the concepts of 'left' and 'right' in locations.

Evaluating coursebooks

Coursebooks are evaluated and adapted informally all the time both by teachers and learners. Teachers monitor what works and what does not work and add their own style and interpretation to the book. Coursebooks can also be evaluated formally. One obvious aim of such evaluation could be for teachers to put a case to school administration to change an old coursebook or to identify ways in which the given coursebook can be supplemented. Coursebook evaluation usually starts with examining the author's claims about the book. For example, if it is claimed that the coursebook gives all four skills an equal balance or includes systematic learner training, or teaches reading with authentic, fun texts, these claims can be checked easily by examining the relevant units in the book. In addition to the coursebook author's original claims, each and every teaching/learning context will generate a set of additional criteria that are important to the specific teachers, children, and schools. These criteria can be divided into three different sets of factors, as shown in Table 9.1.

Teachers will evaluate and select coursebooks according to how appropriate they seem for the given context. For example, where the learners are very young (four to five years of age) and the teachers are inexperienced, it may be advisable to look for a coursebook that 1) contains songs, rhymes, and action stories with drama and hands-on crafts for this very young age group, and 2) supports the inexperienced teachers by providing detailed teachers' notes including sample language used in the classrooms, tips, explanations, answer keys to exercises, full tapescripts, ideas, and activities in photocopiable sheets to use in the classes. Well designed teachers' books can support inexperienced teachers a great deal because they act as training materials.

Learner factors	These factors include the age, cultural background, cognitive maturity, interests, and needs of the learners.
Teacher factors	These factors include teachers' professional background, whether they are native or non-native teachers, their experience in a given context, typical workload, way of working, difficulties and interests, and their access to professional development opportunities.
Institutional and contextual factors	These factors include the number and frequency of hours English is taught per week, how English is integrated into the rest of the curriculum, whether there are curricular guidelines, the resources available to teachers and learners such as computers, access to the Internet, tapes, videos, story book collections, and restrictions such as furniture that cannot be moved in the English classrooms.

Table 9.1: Drawing up criteria for coursebook evaluation

Textbooks can also be evaluated by exploring teachers' and learners' experiences and opinions of them as used in the classroom. It is possible to give questionnaires to or interview learners or other colleagues to find out what aspects of the book they like or do not like and why, and what does or does not suit their contexts. Findings from such interviews and questionnaires and possible observations by outsiders as to how the book is used in class can reveal interesting results about the effectiveness of a coursebook. Children's and teachers' opinions about the same coursebook can sometimes be different or change over time, so it is important for teachers to monitor their own experience as well as the children's opinions and experiences. Since it is impossible to find the perfect coursebook, most teachers will engage in activities to supplement and refresh the one they are working with.

Teachers often change the focus of an activity in the coursebook, or add or take away a step from the suggested procedures to make the activity work better for their classes. Sometimes they may add more personalization or simplify something. These small adaptations are often spontaneous and occur as a result of teachers' moment-by-moment decision making in class.

Supplementing coursebooks

All coursebooks have attractive features but equally they are all restrictive in some ways. It is important that teachers can take time to identify gaps in their coursebooks. Having done this, they can begin to adapt and rewrite materials to fill these gaps so that the book becomes better suited to their class. Teachers may want to supplement the main coursebook for a number of different reasons. When, for example, an international textbook is used, local teachers may feel that the cultural input is not entirely appropriate. They can adapt existing activities to broaden the cultural perspective by including concerns of local or international interest. For example, rather than discussing festivals in English-speaking countries only, they can compare and include festivals in their own or other countries as well. Another reason to supplement a book may be that the teacher wants to experiment with encouraging children in 'learning to learn'. If 'learning to learn' does not feature in the coursebook, teachers may plan activities to introduce the 'plan–do–review cycle' into each unit or teach specific vocabulary learning strategies. Yet another common reason for supplementing a coursebook is to use attractive authentic materials to motivate learners. For example, a teacher may decide to include authentic stories or story books to supplement the predictable language of the textbook. Story books, children's magazines, and other children's publications as well as the Internet are great sources of authentic materials for teachers.

Adapting authentic texts

One commonly experienced difficulty, especially at lower levels, is associated with the linguistic demands of authentic texts. Children would be very interested in the authentic stories teachers come across, but their language level in English is often not adequate to access these texts in their original form. One useful skill that the teacher can easily develop over time is making judgements about changing and adapting authentic or difficult texts to suit the competence level of the class. In this process it is important to make sure that the original appeal of the text does not suffer. In some cases changing and simplifying can destroy the original. The following section contains two examples showing how adapting authentic texts sometimes works, but sometimes does not.

Adapting a well known fable

The text in Extract 22 can be simplified quite easily. It is a traditional fable (Clark 1990). Fables are particular types of animal stories with moral lessons applicable to human life. This one is about the grasshopper and the ants. In the fable whilst the grasshopper sings and dances all summer, the ants work hard and collect food for the winter. When winter comes, the grasshopper has no food and has to beg the ants to give him some. This fable could be a good source of language learning for children, but as indicated by a teacher below, the traditional English version of Aesop's (Greek) fable is far too difficult for her class of eight-year-olds with very little English.

This teacher has crossed out words and phrases such as 'unexpectedly', 'spread out', and 'store' and also replaced some phrases with simpler ones such as 'began to bring out their food' instead of 'began to spread out their store'. After crossing out the words, she made further changes to the text by inserting repetition to make the content more accessible to her children. The text now resembles the cumulative stories described in Chapter 5. In this version (see Table 9.2 overleaf) the grasshopper talks to several ants and each time the conversation is the same. The grasshopper says he is hungry and asks for food, and the ants ask him what he was doing in the summer. When they find out that he was idle, they do not give him any food. This pattern is repeated with predictable language. The teacher has also changed the story ending. The ants refuse to give the grasshopper any food but when the queen ant comes along she suggests a solution. They give him food but they make him promise that he will help next year and will play music for them all year round.

Fables

The grasshopper and the ants

One winter day, when the sun came out unexpectedly, all the

ants hurried out of their anthill and began to spread out their
food ?
store of grain to dry.   *bring out*

Up came the grasshopper who said: 'I am so hungry. Please,

will you give some of your grain?'

One of the ants stopped working for a moment and replied:

'Why should we? What has happened to your own ~~store of~~ food

for the winter?'
any
'I have not got a ~~store~~' - said the grasshopper. 'I did not have

time to collect any food last summer because I spent the whole

time singing.'

The ant laughed and all the others joined in.

'If you spent the summer singing, you will have to spend the

winter dancing for your supper.'

The grasshopper went on his way, hungry.

Extract 22 (Clark 1990)

One winter day the grasshopper met an ant. The ant was eating some nice food.
The grasshopper said, 'I am so hungry. Can you give me some food, please?'
The ant said, 'I worked hard all summer. What did you do in the summer, grasshopper?'
'I was singing and dancing.'
The ant shook her head and did not give him any food.
The grasshopper was very sad and hungry. He met another ant.
The grasshopper said, 'I am so hungry. Can you give me some food, please?'
The ant said, 'I worked hard all summer. What did you do in the summer, grasshopper?'
'I was singing and dancing.'
The ant shook her head and did not give him any food.
The grasshopper was sad and hungry when he met a third ant.
The grasshopper said, 'I am so hungry. Can you give me some food, please?'
The ant said, 'I worked hard all summer. What did you do in the summer, grasshopper?'
'I was singing and dancing.'
The ant shook her head and did not give him any food.
The grasshopper was sad and hungry when he met the queen of the ants.
The grasshopper said, 'I am so hungry. Can you give me some food, please?'
The queen said, 'I worked hard all summer. What did you do in the summer, grasshopper?'
'I was singing and dancing.'
The queen said, 'I see. We will give you some food but you have to promise to help us next summer and play music for us all year around.'
The grasshopper was happy and he promised to help and play music for them.
He had a nice dinner with his new friends.

Table 9.2: Adaptation of 'The Grasshopper and the Ants' for storytelling

This adaptation, although in the end quite dramatically different from the original, still works for a number of reasons. First of all the story is still a good source for learning new vocabulary, structures, and functions. Children can learn names of animals, listen to the past tense used in narrative, and learn the questions and answer routine from the conversations between the grasshopper and the ants. The traditional moral lesson taught by this fable about the need to work for your food is still there, although changing it slightly makes the message less harsh. Children can listen to or read the story about the grasshopper and the ants with enjoyment; they can act it out, and certainly learn some English from it.

Adapting does not always work

My second example, however, shows that adaptation does not always work. Extract 23 is an authentic piece of text from *The Jolly Postman* by Janet and

---

MEENY, MINY, MO & CO., SOLICITORS
Alley O Buildings, Toe Lane, Tel: 12345.

Dear Mr Wolf,

We are writing to you on behalf of our
client, Miss Riding-Hood, concerning her
grandma. Miss Hood tells us that you
are presently occupying her grandma's
cottage and wearing her grandma's clothes
without this lady's permission.

Please understand that if this harassment
does not cease, we will call in the Official
Woodcutter, and - if necessary - all the
King's horses and all the King's men.

On a separate matter, we must inform you
that Messrs. Three Little Pigs Ltd. are
now firmly resolved to sue for damages.
Your offer of shares in a turnip or
apple-picking business is declined, and
all this huffing and puffing will get
you nowhere.

Yours sincerely,

Harold Meeny

H Meeny

Extract 23 (Ahlberg and Ahlberg 1986)

Allen Ahlberg. This is an interesting story book in which the main character is a postman who delivers letters and cards written by characters from traditional English stories, rhymes, and songs. This text is a letter written by a solicitor to the Wolf on behalf of Little Red Riding Hood, the famous story character who went to see her grandmother. Whilst this is a very amusing piece of authentic text, it is full of references to many other stories and characters, not just Little Red Riding Hood. Children would only be able to appreciate it if all these references were made clear. In addition to this difficulty, the letter is written using complicated 'pretend legal' language.

Taking out the references to other stories or replacing the legal terms would not work because the humour and charm of this piece of text are deeply embedded in the language use and references. My advice with such texts would be not to use them at all or to use them only if they are accessible to children without any adaptation and simplification.

Adapting materials in this way can make a range of authentic texts accessible to children with little English. It is, however, important to recognize that adapting authentic texts excessively denies children the pleasure and the challenge of tackling real English. This is why it is wise not to overdo it. Teachers who adapt materials may want to try authentic texts or sometimes make a conscious effort to move gradually from a great deal of adaptation to less as their class learn to cope with more challenges. Using authentic texts encourages children to guess vocabulary from context and make use of other clues such as illustrations. It is important to remember that they do not need to understand everything to enjoy such texts. Authentic materials can be a great source of interest and motivation for young learners but it is important that challenge and support are balanced. Adapting original texts is certainly a way of supporting children and allowing them to access a wider range of materials.

Creating own materials

Topic-based planning

In many primary schools where English is integrated with other areas of the curriculum, teachers integrate planning for English into their general planning. Many primary schools use what we call 'topic-based planning', which means that a topic is chosen for a term and all the activities in all areas of the curriculum will be related to that one broad topic. For example, if the topic is 'Water', in maths children might measure how much water goes into different containers, in geography they might take a trip to the local pond and observe the life of water creatures, in art they might look at famous paintings of the sea, and in English they might write simple poems about water. Topic-based learning is beneficial and meaningful because all new learning experiences are deeply rooted in the same theme and children can see the links between various learning tasks and areas of learning. This is conducive to a holistic approach to learning. The difficulty from the perspective of teachers is that this type of planning is very time-consuming and without a clear linear outline it is difficult to ensure that all objectives are covered by the end of the year.

Topic-based planning and teaching is also popular among teachers of English who have the freedom to plan their own materials. Once the topic is selected, teachers will typically brainstorm activities and games that can be used to introduce the new language related to that topic in a natural way. Table 9.3 and Figure 9.1 illustrate how teachers might start brainstorming ideas for the topic of 'Families' in their English class.

UNIT: FAMILIES

Younger learners	Older learners
• *Cross-curricular activity* Crafting: a family tree: make the tree, decorate it, display it, and talk about it • *Vocabulary* members of the family (with extended family) • *Structure* 'have got' • *Listening* Short descriptions of families in different parts of the world • *Speaking* dialogues: Sharing photo albums: 'This is my brother. He is two here.' • *Listening* Animal families • *Crafting* Making cards for Mothers' Day or Fathers' Day	• *Reading* sections of an authentic book: Children like you in the world (an information book) • *Speaking* Future of families in our societies • *Mind maps* Advantages and disadvantages of having big families • *Speaking* Family you would like when you grow up • *Structure* 'When I grow up, I will' • *Listening* Extraordinary families • *Writing* Introduce your family – create a webpage • *Speaking* Play a game: Find someone who … in their family.

Table 9.3: Ideas for younger and older children on the topic of Families

Figure 9.1: Activities on the topic of Families

Lesson planning

Once some ideas for activities have been brainstormed, the next step is to think carefully about the objectives for each activity and begin to sequence them. Table 9.4 shows a draft plan to teach three consecutive lessons to children aged seven using some of the ideas from the table above. Each lesson is 40 minutes long, and has a main objective and a number of steps. Each step takes about ten minutes, which leaves time for a warmer at the beginning and a closing activity at the end. All three lessons are focused on listening and speaking because these children do not yet do any reading or writing.

Lesson 1 (40 minutes)	Lesson 2 (40 minutes)	Lesson 3 (40 minutes)
Objective(s) Introduce members of family vocabulary (mother, father, sister, brother, etc.) and 'have got'.	**Objective(s)** Further practice of 'have got' + family members + introduce question form 'have you got'?	**Objective(s)** Introduce vocabulary for animal families and consolidate language from lessons 1 and 2.
Steps 1 **Listen** to a short text where a child describes a photo album: **match pictures with names of family** members in pairs (exposure to 'have got'). 2 **Snap card game:** (introduce sample language): practise names of family members in groups ('I have got' + family members). 3 **Drama:** (model) acting out family members (ask children to freeze when music stops).	*Steps* 1 **Family chant** joining in. 2 **Team game: Listen to descriptions of families:** two teams: children listen and run to stick cards on the board when they hear the names of family members (model rules). 3 **Mingling game:** find somebody who (has two sisters, has a brother, has three cousins, etc.). Model sample question/answer routine.	*Steps* 1 **Song: Animal families** joining in with miming. 2 **Gap speaking task:** children are given cards with pictures of family members and pets to describe for each other to complete families (model question and answer routines). 3 **Craft:** Making family trees or family posters including pets (provide models). Each child can choose one craft activity. In the next lesson they will talk about their posters and family trees.

Table 9.4: Lesson planning

During the process of planning it is a good idea to keep these questions in mind:

1 Do the lessons fit together well? (Is there a logical progression from one lesson to the next? Does my second lesson build on my first lesson?)

2 Do the lessons look balanced in terms of variety of activities, skills, interaction patterns? (Is there a range of activities, are both listening and speaking practised and is there any group or pair work?)

3 Do I have a progression from receptive to productive practice (listen first and then speak)?

4 Are the activities meaningful for the children? Why will they want to do them?

5 Is the language outcome real, natural? Is the sample language planned for the activities real and meaningful? Would children use the language like this in the real world?

6 Are all the activities different? Check that no two activities do exactly the same thing.

7 Have I thought of optional activities for those pairs/groups or individuals who finish early?

8 Have I included my usual warmers/closing activities such as homework check?

9 Have I included timing for each activity?

Immediately after teaching a lesson, it is a good idea to take a few minutes to think about how the plan worked out, what went well and why in order to improve the planning process on subsequent occasions.

Writing own texts

As part of working on a topic, it is possible to exploit stories, poems, songs, and rhymes, too. Many teachers enjoy writing their own stories, songs, and rhymes. Here is a rhyme/song a group of teachers from Russia created on the topic of 'Food'.

> I eat apples –
> Crunch, crunch, crunch.
> I eat sandwiches –
> Munch, munch, munch.
> I eat lollipops –
> Lick, lick, lick.
> And I eat ice cream –
> Quick, quick, quick.

Children can also contribute ideas to add to or change texts such as story endings. With some support, they can create their own poems, rhymes, or stories. Practice leads to enjoyment and more creativity for both teachers and children.

Summary

In this chapter materials evaluation has been discussed taking coursebooks as a starting point. Teachers might want to supplement their coursebooks with authentic materials taken from story books, the Internet, or other sources. Teachers' creativity and their confidence is the real driving force to supplement the coursebook or write new materials for the class. The involvement of children is important both in evaluating coursebooks and choosing and creating new materials.

Recommended reading

Background theory

Brewster, J., G. Ellis, and **D. Girard.** 2002. *The Primary English Teacher's Guide* (2nd edn.) Part 3: A World of Resources. Harlow: Pearson Limited.

This particular chapter explores the opportunities teachers in primary language classrooms may have when it comes to exploring resources around them, including authentic materials.

Cunningsworth, A. 1995. *Choosing Your Course Book.* Oxford: Macmillan.

This is a useful book which offers advice on how to create coursebook evaluation checklists and how to use them to select the most suitable book for a particular context.

Tomlinson, B. (ed.). 2003. *Developing Materials for Language Teachers.* London: Continuum Cromwell Press.

This book summarizes the principles and procedures of materials development, including electronic materials, visual elements, and materials for different learner groups. It also has a special section about the role of materials development in teacher training.

Tomlinson, B. (ed.). 1998. *Materials Development in Language Teaching.* Cambridge: Cambridge University Press.

This book contains chapters by distinguished authors in the area of materials design in ELT. There are chapters on how to collect data for materials writing, how to go about the process of writing course materials for specific learner groups, and how to evaluate them.

Practical teacher resources

Moon, J. 2000. *Children Learning English.* Chapters 7 and 9. Oxford: Macmillan.

These two chapters contain many useful ideas for teachers in primary English classes who are in the position to create their own teaching materials. Chapter 7 offers a checklist for creating language learning activities and Chapter 9 introduces the idea of topic-based planning with its benefits and disadvantages. There is clear advice about sequencing activities, too.

Tasks

If you would like to look at some practical tasks to explore your own practice related to the content of this chapter, you can try Tasks 12: Planning lessons and 13: Exploring authentic materials (Appendix pages 161 and 162).

10 ASSESSMENT

Introduction

All teachers need to know how effective their teaching is and all learners are interested in how well they are doing. Assessment of the learning process is therefore an integral part of teaching and learning. In the case of children, however, traditional assessment methods can be problematic. This is why it is important that assessment in language learning for children is handled with care. This chapter will introduce some child-friendly methods that can be used in a variety of different contexts, preferably in combination with each other.

Purposes of assessment

Assessment refers to the process of data analysis that teachers use to get evidence about their learners' performance and progress in English. In terms of purpose, assessment is carried out because head teachers, school authorities, and parents require evidence of learning but it is also the right of the children to know how they are doing.

All teachers want to be able to check whether students are achieving the target objectives. Teachers are concerned with what the students will be able to do, say, or write as a result of their teaching. For example, after completing a unit on 'Families', the children will be able to talk or write a short paragraph about their own families. They may also be able to answer questions about their families and talk about their photo albums. They will be able to recite a rhyme or sing a song from the same unit. It is important for teachers to identify these objectives at the beginning of each unit of teaching so that they can check children's performance against them. Teachers will be able to see where the gaps are, what seems easier or harder for a group of learners, and what objectives have been achieved by everyone. These findings will feed directly into everyday teaching. For example, teachers may spend more time on those aspects of the unit that proved to be harder or they might spend some time looking again at an activity which was seen to be problematic in an assessment exercise. The main aim of this process, called formative assessment, is to inform and improve teaching. In addition to formative assessment, teachers also need to engage in summative assessment, which means taking stock of what has been learnt and achieved at the end of a longer period, for example, at the end of a course or a year. Summative assessment is often associated with a certificate of some kind.

Assessment of young learners

Why are traditional methods problematic?

As stated in the introduction, assessing young learners can be problematic. Young children's knowledge of English often comprises, for example, being able to sing songs, participate in stories and games, mime an action story, i.e. things that are not easy and straightforward to assess objectively. Traditional 'paper and pencil tests' typically include activities such as filling in gaps in sentences, answering multiple choice questions, or translating vocabulary lists. They are often favoured by teachers because they are relatively easy to set and correct and they reduce language knowledge to points, marks, and grades, i.e. quantifiable results. However, in the case of younger children especially, these tests often do not work because such isolated exercises do not show what children know and can do with confidence. They might also have a negative influence on teaching so that instead of singing, reciting rhymes, listening to stories, and playing games, children will have to spend time answering multiple choice questions in class in order to prepare for the test. This is often called the negative washback effect of tests. Children are often not yet very good at writing and this means that traditional tests can be stressful and tiring. There is the danger that inappropriate assessment methods and possibly lower grades would discourage children and cause them to lose their motivation to learn English. Given that many programmes aim to develop attitudinal goals such as positive motivation towards language learning and broadening cultural horizons, these tests could do more harm than good.

Gap between teaching and testing?

Pauline Rea-Dickins and Shelagh Rixon, two British researchers with interest both in young learners learning English and in testing, published some intriguing results about primary English teachers' beliefs and practices with regard to assessment. This questionnaire survey in 1999 showed that a great majority of primary English teachers in many parts of the world used 'paper and pencil tests' as major tools of assessment. The sample tests provided by the respondents revealed that they used a narrow range of grammar and vocabulary tests in single sentence exercises. For example, the most commonly used items were either matching two items of vocabulary, providing an equivalent in the first language, or gap-filling. All operations seemed to be at the level of single sentences. With regard to testing the language skills, it was found that the two skills that seemed to be tested extensively were reading and writing, though only at sentence level. The assessment of listening skills was not mentioned at all, even though it is one of the foundation skills in the primary classroom. Testing speaking was restricted to reciting rehearsed dialogues. Rea-Dickins and Rixon comment that testing practices like these convey a strange message to children about the nature of language and communication. Children's natural capacities to work out meaning from rich language input were not taken into account when these assessment tools were designed. In their conclusion, the authors argue that there is a need for teachers in primary English classes to go beyond paper and pencil tests and explore alternative approaches which engage learners more appropriately, for example, with language beyond the sentence level through listening. They also say however that teachers need opportunities to understand the assessment culture of their contexts as well as training and support in familiarizing themselves with various assessment practices and techniques.

Child-friendly methods

It is important for teachers to use assessment techniques that are child-friendly and compatible with the activities used every day in their classrooms. In order to understand what children have learnt, teachers may need to use a variety of assessment methods. If traditional pencil and paper tests need to be used because of institutional restrictions, they should be considered together with other methods such as self-assessment, portfolio assessment, or observations, in order to get a more complete and more reliable picture of children's achievements.

There are two main approaches to assessment: norm referencing and criterion referencing. Norm referencing means that teachers compare their learners' achievement with the norm, i.e. the class average. If someone is below average, they will get a low mark. One problem is that this approach to assessment fails to take into account small individual progress and achievements, and it encourages comparison and competition among children. Criterion referencing, on the other hand, means that learners have to meet certain set criteria. Teachers make a note of where each learner is according to the criteria and then track their progress. All children can progress at their own pace. Comparisons among children are discouraged because individual achievement is in focus. Children's results and achievements are compared with their starting point. In criterion referencing, teachers of young learners tend to favour success-oriented assessment, i.e. they encourage and praise everybody and value both efforts and achievement. Children carry out tasks in familiar learning contexts in an environment that encourages confidence and builds self-esteem and as a result they are not worried about being assessed.

Assessment techniques

Many coursebooks recommend their own set of assessment materials, and schools and institutions may have their own well established assessment systems. Within a school context, whether English is integrated into the primary curriculum or taught separately, the assessment culture of the school will influence the assessment practices in English. For example, in schools where eight-year-olds are assessed in every subject with a single grade (1–5), it is unlikely that it will be possible to follow a different system for English. In these contexts it is often the case that teachers work on compromises such as respecting the grade system but awarding only good grades for both effort and achievement. Teachers can choose from a range of alternative assessment tools, most of which can be incorporated into the teaching practice of any context.

Observation

Teachers can use systematic observation as a tool to assess children's performances. Observation is non-intrusive because children are often not even aware that they are being assessed. The same sort of task is given to children in class again and again until they are used to it and then the teacher observes the performance of a particular group. Depending on the goals of the observation, teachers can assess children in a variety of situations such as working in pairs or groups or independently. Observation is also good for checking the performance of non-linguistic skills (such as engagement, interest, motivation) which make up some of the core objectives of primary English programmes. Simple observation checklists can be created for these purposes. Many coursebooks suggest their own checklists. The example of an oral assessment observation checklist in Extract 24 is taken from *New English Parade 1*.

This particular checklist leaves spaces in the columns on the left for the teachers to fill in the names of relevant activities such as 1) pairs acting out a role-play, or 2) pairs doing a Spot the Differences task, or 3) individuals talking about their photo albums. The children's names are entered at the top. Finally, the teacher enters one of the three categories: 'C' for competent, 'N' for not competent yet, and 'W' for working on it. It is of course

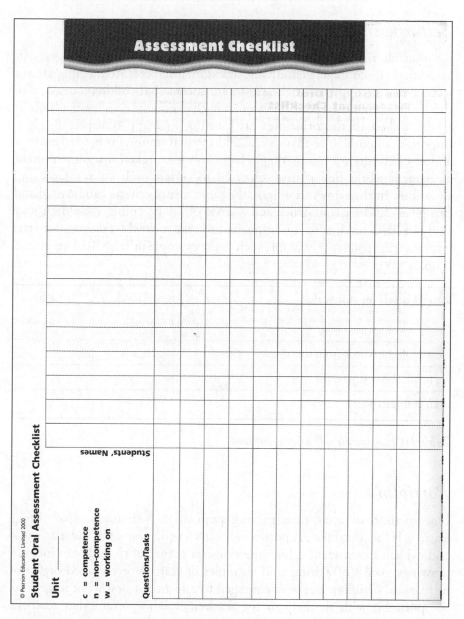

Extract 24 (Zanatta and Herrera 2000)

important that teachers decide what criteria they are using to award C as opposed to W or N. Different pairs and groups with N can be observed again until they achieve 'C'. Some children will take longer to get to the competent stage. Checklists can be developed for other tasks such as writing or reading, listening, or 'learning to learn' activities.

Self-assessment

Another alternative method that teachers can experiment with is self-assessment. Encouraging children to assess themselves is an integral part of a learner-centred approach. Self-assessment means that children are asked to think about their own performances and achievements on a regular basis. It is also linked to the principles of 'learning to learn' (Chapter 8). It is important to emphasize that careful and gradual training is needed and the ability of children to assess themselves cannot be taken for granted. Self-assessment works best if it is restricted to certain well known tasks and situations. In the same sort of task, the same sort of criteria can be used and this gives children confidence and a sense of safety. Younger children may find this harder at first so it is important to take it slowly. Teachers can start with something relatively simple such as the example in Table 10.1 and build it up.

Rate yourself on this scale	Very good ★★★★	Good ★★	Try again ★
I learnt all the words from this unit.			
I can talk about my family.			
I can count to 50.			

Table 10.1: A simple self-assessment tool

Portfolio

One method of assessment gaining popularity with teachers of young learners is the 'portfolio'. A portfolio means a collection of a student's work and evidence of student achievement over a period of time. It can include drawings, pieces of writing, and examples of crafts or even taped oral performances. Children can be encouraged to select their best work to go into the portfolio with the help of the teacher. It is important that teachers together with the children work out criteria for selection, otherwise some children might want to put in everything without developing the ability to differentiate between samples of work. Children's growing ability to choose examples they think show their ability at best is linked to their ability to reflect about their learning. If children are used to reflecting about their work on a regular basis as part of the 'learning to learn' activities integrated into the English class, then they will find using a portfolio both natural and meaningful.

In addition to the sample pieces of work, portfolios can be used for collecting information about children's activities outside the classroom. Pages can be inserted to prompt them to think about what they want to learn next and why. These may include pages which get them to summarize and reflect on what they can do in English, i.e. self-assessment pages. The example in Extract 25, referring to the reading skill, has been taken from a Council of Europe publication on *Language Portfolios for Children*. The left-hand side suggests children colour in the bubbles when they think they can read the texts listed. The right-hand side offers a much more detailed account of the process of developing sub-skills in reading. This is then supplemented by the learners' own selection of texts they can read or reading tasks they have completed.

Portfolios link teaching and assessment very clearly since they offer concrete evidence of what a learner can do. This method of assessment can also motivate learners by getting them to focus on what they are good at and develop ownership of the learning process, thus promoting learner independence. However, portfolios are arguably labour intensive from the teacher's point of view especially if the teacher helps with the process of selection and gives ample feedback at regular times both in writing and sitting down with individual children. In the case of younger children teachers may have to take more responsibility for helping to choose appropriate pieces of work. Portfolios can be bulky and they need to be stored somewhere where the children can have easy access to them. It is also important that rules are worked out about taking them home. Parents can take an active part in promoting their children's learning by taking an interest in their portfolios.

Project work

Many teachers like to use project work as an alternative tool for assessment. If children often work in groups during the lesson then it is logical to assess them in groups, too. The advantage of this tool is that it combines all four language skills and the joint effort of several children. Working together with others and completing a substantial task can be very motivating for weaker learners because of the opportunities to learn from friends. It is also beneficial for stronger learners because they have a chance to display their knowledge and skills. Projects can work well in mixed ability classes if the members of the groups are carefully selected and all have appropriately defined roles and tasks and adhere to agreed rules. In addition, project work is an opportunity for children to demonstrate other non-linguistic strengths such as drawing or acting. There is of course the disadvantage that it is very difficult to assign grades to project work because of the need to acknowledge both individual work and group effort, and it is virtually impossible to be

Extract 25 (Council of Europe 2001)

my language
BIOGRAPHY

GETTING BETTER!

What I can do in:

reading   ✔

I can read aloud and understand some words, which we have practised.	
I can match some simple words and pictures.	
I can read and understand short sentences, which we have practised.	
I can read and understand some rhymes and poems.	
I can use my book or a vocabulary to find out what some new words mean.	
I can read and understand short messages such as e-mails and postcards.	
I can read and say which are the most important parts of passages from a book.	
I can use a dictionary to look up new words.	
I can read and understand longer passages from a book.	
I am beginning to read short stories, which the teacher has already read aloud to me and can use clues to guess the meaning of new words.	
I can read and understand lots of different texts, some about the past, present or future.	
I can read and understand the key points in some real things like magazine and newspapers articles, leaflets and letters.	

Other

completely fair to everyone. One solution is to give children praise and general feedback rather than grades and use project work as part of formative assessment. Teachers might want to experiment with grouping children in various ways to find out which groups work best for collaborative learning. This could easily lead to an action research project and interesting discoveries. (See Chapter 11 on action research.)

Combining assessment instruments

In many contexts, in addition to ongoing assessment, teachers use summative assessment at the end of the primary programme. It was mentioned in Chapter 4 that continuity between primary and secondary primary programmes is very important and therefore a reliable assessment tool which can measure children's knowledge and skills in English is a great asset.

In some countries there are initiatives to introduce summative assessment at the end of primary English programmes. For example, in Norway, the Ministry of Education successfully piloted a national assessment project with primary learners at the end of the sixth grade (age 11–12). In a paper published in 2000, Angela Hasselgren, a researcher at the University of Bergen, explained their initiative. In Norway their aim was to help teachers assess their learners' strengths and weaknesses with multiple forms of assessment including self-assessment. A whole package was designed because more tools can measure children's abilities more fully. The design of this assessment package took into account a number of restrictions. First of all, children had only limited experience of writing. Secondly, the curriculum guidelines for English were rather loose so teachers were covering different things in different schools. Finally, teachers and learners alike had little experience of alternative assessment tools so the test had to be easy to manage with lots of pictures and other visuals. In order to achieve a positive washback effect, they also had to promote good learning. The actual package consisted of four episodes of a cartoon-picture mystery story about a hunt for a lost circus elephant. The tool was trialled extensively in Norwegian primary schools and the results indicated that children became very engaged in the tasks and genuinely used their skills to solve the mystery. Some of the tasks were done collaboratively in small groups. Learners were asked to score their own performance using simple self-assessment charts. The instrument included a great variety of tasks, such as picture description, matching sentences, or listening to someone talking about circus life. The most important principle that they followed was that multiple perspectives of learners' performance were more reliable than one-off tests. Teachers' assessment of the children was interpreted together with students' self-assessment comments and both parties found working with the assessment package a very positive experience. Teachers found that overall most pupils were realistic about assessing their own skills.

Summary

In the case of children, traditional scores and paper and pencil tests do not work especially if they are used as the only method of assessment. A variety of principles have been suggested for introducing alternative assessment methods into TEYL classrooms. Assessment does not have to be stressful and competitive. Instead, it can contribute to fostering positive self-image and self-esteem in a collaborative environment.

Recommended reading

Background theory

Carpenter, K., N. Fujii, and **H. Kataoka.** 1995. 'An oral interview procedure for assessing second language abilities in children' *Language Testing* 12/2: 157–181.

A summary of empirical research conducted in the United States to work out how to design and standardize oral assessment for young learners.

Language Testing Special Issue 2000. 17:2

This whole issue of the *Language Testing* journal is devoted to assessment with young learners. The volume contains several articles from different contexts exploring issues such as purposes and methods of assessment for children learning languages in the primary school.

Practical teacher resources

Ioannou-Georgiou, S. and **P. Pavlou.** 2003. *Assessing Young Learners* (Resource Books for Teachers). Oxford: Oxford University Press.

This is a collection of imaginative assessment ideas and activities to use in primary classrooms. The book contains multiple assessment techniques such as portfolio, self-assessment, and project work but also more traditional assessment techniques carefully explained and classified for different age groups.

Tasks

If you would like to look at some practical tasks to explore your own practice related to the content of this chapter, you can try Task 14: 'Designing your own learning materials' (Appendix page 163).

11 RESEARCH IN THE PRIMARY ENGLISH CLASSROOM

Introduction

As part of their teaching, most teachers reflect on what they and their learners are doing and why, and thus continuously explore their own classrooms and their own practice. They may take a mental note of what did and did not work and what the children seemed to enjoy. Such initially informal explorations, if undertaken on a systematic basis, can naturally lead teachers to engage in classroom research to discover more about themselves, their learners, and the complexities of their classrooms. The main aim of this chapter is to give some guidelines to teachers who wish to engage in explorations of their own classrooms in a systematic way. As part of this process, teachers may wish to focus on themselves or on their learners, or on any aspect of their teaching. Since the learners are children, the second aim of this chapter is to discuss aspects of research methodology specific to child rather than adult subjects.

Classroom research

In previous chapters it has already been emphasized that the teacher plays a crucial part in the process of children's foreign language learning. For example, I have stressed the teacher's role in providing varied language input, in motivating and encouraging learners, in monitoring learners' interests by adjusting materials and activities to their needs, and in developing 'learning to learn' skills. Teachers can and should be encouraged to take initiatives, make decisions for themselves, and adapt materials and activities for their specific circumstances. This approach of course also implies that teachers monitor and develop their own understanding of teaching and learning on an ongoing basis. Trying to find answers to questions that arise in the classroom is part of everyday teaching. Explorations, reflections, and readiness to change are therefore principles that remain at the core of all good teaching.

Action research cycles

Classroom research or action research are types of research that are typically initiated by classroom practitioners. The special characteristic of this type of research is that the results provide answers that are of immediate importance to teachers. They explore their own practice with the aim of improving some aspects of their teaching and thus positively influencing the quality of learning in the classroom. This type of research is context-specific and small-scale and, as such, cannot be generalized beyond the given context/classroom. Teachers often work collaboratively with colleagues on research projects of common interest. Many teachers find that in collaboration with others they can learn more, encourage each other, and sustain motivation for their chosen focus. During the process of exploring a question, they engage in critical reflection about their teaching and their classrooms and share and develop ideas together. Figure 11.1 shows the reflective cycle, which contains the following steps: a teacher or a group of teachers will start by selecting a focus, a question, an issue, or a problem. The next step is to find appropriate instruments to investigate that focus. Then they collect and analyse data from their classrooms. After that, they reflect on the results and develop an action plan for what changes need to be made. The next step is to implement the change and observe the effects. Often the process cannot finish here because new issues and questions arise from the new situation and the teacher/teachers have new questions to ask and thus initiate a new cycle of research. This is why action research is often described as a cyclical process.

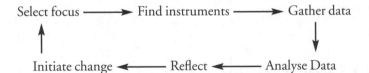

Figure 11.1: The reflective cycle

There follow some examples of issues and questions a teacher or a group of teachers in the primary EYL classroom may want to explore in an action research project. These questions are grouped according to what type of instrument would be required to find answers. Some questions could be explored by observation of the children working together, while others would require that teachers find out what the children are thinking. Yet other questions can be explored by audio or video recording lessons or inviting an observer to take notes.

Focus on children: observations

Observation is one of the most commonly used research methods with children. Many questions and issues in TEYL classroom can be explored by using systematic observation. Here are some possible examples.

- When they can choose partners, who do children choose to work with? Does this pattern change over the course of the year?
- What types of pair work tasks are suitable for younger age groups, for example, six-year-olds?
- What types of tasks do six-year-olds and ten-year-olds enjoy?

To begin to explore these issues the teacher may want to do some structured observation. For example, in the first question, whenever the children are allowed to choose activities for themselves, the teacher can take a note of who is working with whom, how many children work in groups, and who is working alone. A simple observation sheet such as the one in Figure 11.2 would be suitable.

Date	Individuals	Pairs	Groups	Comment
	Clare	Zoe and Mark	Tim, William, and Andrea	
	Steve checks what Bethany and Thomas are doing and then returns to his own chair.	Bethany and Thomas		

Figure 11.2: A simple observation schedule

As part of their everyday teaching, teachers informally observe children all the time. A teacher may want to focus the observation on a group of children, on one particular individual, or on the whole class.

Initial informal observation may lead to other methods and tools. For example, let us imagine that some teachers are interested in the motivational sources of particular learners, perhaps because they are highly motivated or because they are not motivated at all. In the first case teachers may want to find out about the factors that contribute to their learners' high levels of motivation and in the second case they may want to explore ways in which children with low levels of motivation can be helped to change. As a first step teachers may want to talk to the children and then decide to observe them in a variety of situations, for example, working on their own, with others in a group, or during whole class activities. Colleagues could be asked to join the class and help with the observation. When exploring something as complex as motivation, it is especially important to base judgement on several observations in different contexts rather than just one.

Focus on children: asking about their views and opinions

In the above example asking children's opinions was one possible instrument for exploration. Here are some other examples where teachers might want to talk to children.

- Which activities do children enjoy and why? Do they enjoy project work as much as I do?
- Which activities do they find difficult?
- Do they like the book? Do they use the book after school?
- How do they perceive their own knowledge and skills in the second language?
- What are their sources of motivation at different ages?
- What strategies do children use to remember new vocabulary?

Asking about children's views and opinions is consistent with the philosophy advocated in this book, that teachers need to find out as much as possible about their learners so that they can adjust their teaching to children's changing needs. It is important for teachers to talk to children informally to find out about their needs, interests, and views. In addition, teachers can attempt to explore children's ideas and opinions on a systematic basis rather than just during informal conversations. However, teachers need to take special care when designing, choosing, and administering these instruments and interpreting the results.

Using interviews

One instrument often used to find out about what children feel or think about different issues is the interview. When teachers interview children, in the great majority of cases children's first language will of course have to be used. Interviewing children can be challenging. One issue to be aware of is that children may find it difficult to explain if something is not clear to them and under pressure, they might give a nonsensical answer rather than saying 'I do not know' or 'I am not sure' or 'Can you explain this again?' Children might not be able to make sense of the context of the interview, a point raised in Chapter 1 with reference to the work of Margaret Donaldson. Another common problem is that in an interview children often want to please the adult and thus give answers that they think he/she wants to hear. Questions therefore need to be phrased in ways which do not readily reveal expected answers. Many children, especially younger ones, may find answering questions individually too overwhelming. Indeed, some children may refuse to say anything at all. Ann Lewis (1992), a British researcher in child studies and an expert in child research techniques, recommends that, if at all possible, children should be interviewed in groups rather than individually. The make-up of these groups is crucial because children need to feel confident and comfortable with the others in the group. Teachers will need to consider issues of gender, group dynamics, and friendships or other important relationship patterns. Children should never be pressed for answers. Some children in the group might choose not to say anything at all and this has to be accepted by the interviewer. On the other hand, in safe friendship groups, they will more easily open up and offer ideas and thoughts and bounce ideas off each other. There is, however, always the risk that they may respond to peer pressure by saying what the group leader or most popular child thinks.

Children need to have plenty of time to think and answer questions and all kinds of responses should be valued. Teachers can start with a chat to warm the children up. It is also good to provide relevant prompts, something concrete such as a collection of books if books are the focus, or a worksheet with different activities if we want to ask them about activities they do in class. In my own research (Pinter 2001), which explored how children coped with interactive tasks, I used the videotape of their performances of the tasks to start off the interviews. These prompts are important because they provide a focus and a reminder to the children. To help very young children, it might be advisable to present the questions within the frame of a familiar game or a story or combine the interview with some other familiar activity. Questions can be turned into or be combined with a simple role-play exercise. For example, instead of asking children directly a list of questions about what usually happens when they are learning new vocabulary in class, it is possible to pretend one of them is the teacher and the others are the students. The 'teacher' can then teach the others some new words. By playing the roles, they can show exactly how they make sense of what is happening in their classes and can convey what they find important or meaningful. If this is not appropriate or possible, contextualizing the questions is always a good option. For example, instead of asking 'What makes a good performance on this task?' we can say 'This task will be given to children like you in other schools. Now that you have seen and practised it, what advice would you give to them about how to do well?' This can be more meaningful and their responses may be more enlightening.

Using questionnaires

Questionnaires are better suited for quick factual surveys. Often, question-naires are used together with other methods. They can be used to gather factual data before embarking on face-to-face interviews to get more in-depth data about a particular issue. How can a teacher make sure that questionnaires are effective and fun? Table 11.1 gives some examples which show it is possible to design your own instrument to explore children's insights. When possible, questionnaires are best administered with the teacher present to help and explain as children fill in their responses.

Tick the activity that you want to do again
• Sing a song?
• Listen to a story?
• Make a puppet and talk about it?

Circle your answers
• I like listening to stories
• I am good at reading
• I can count to 100 in English
• I like singing songs in English

Table 11.1: Children's evaluation of activities

The example in Extract 26 is taken from a questionnaire developed by a Korean primary teacher (Park 2002), who was interested in asking children about factors that influenced their English learning. She administered a questionnaire in their mother tongue to children aged seven to 12. This is one of the questions. It illustrates how creative teachers can contextualize questions for children in a way that makes sense to them.

It is important for teachers to check the language used in questionnaires. Children may simply misunderstand a question because they are puzzled by the language used. Even in the first language, the phrasing of the questions needs to be considered very carefully. In my own experience, ten- to 11-year-olds still have considerable difficulty even in their first language with complicated concepts such as 'disadvantage', 'benefit', or 'value'. Another difficulty inherent in questionnaires is the amount of writing and thinking that has to be done. If there are open questions which invite learners to give their own examples and comments, the actual process of writing may be time-consuming and tiring for children who may be inexperienced writers.

13) Suppose that there are four rooms where pupils are studying English. You can see what they are doing in each room through the windows. Which class would you like to join?

☐ *Room 1:* At the beginning of the class the teacher explained what the pupils would learn today. Now the pupils are trying to memorize the new words on the board.

☐ *Room 2:* The pupils are in groups of four and are enthusiastically engaged in discussing a given topic so the room is a bit noisy. The teacher is walking around, answering questions.

☐ *Room 3:* What is said in this room comes only from the teacher. She is speaking in English and the pupils are following her commands without saying a word.

☐ *Room 4:* The pupils loudly repeat the sentences on the board after the teacher. They will practise those sentences chorally and individually for the whole class.

Extract 26 (Park 2002)

Focus on teachers: recording own classroom or inviting an observer

- What interaction patterns are used in my classes?
- How much first language do I use and for what purposes?
- What questions do I ask?
- How can I improve giving simple instructions?
- How much do I talk and how much do the children talk?

There is a lot that teachers may say or do in a classroom that they may be unaware of. Recording one or a series of lessons can provide the teacher with an objective record of exactly what was said, what questions were asked, or what instructions were given. It is impossible to concentrate on everything in every lesson and therefore it is helpful occasionally to choose a focus and explore aspects of one's own practice. In the case of interaction patterns, a colleague might be invited to observe some classes and do a simple count of how many learners answered questions, which learners the teacher nominated, or which learners initiated their own comments. Recording the patterns for one or several lessons will help the teacher to become more aware of what is happening in the classroom. Findings from general, open-ended projects such as 'What is happening in my classroom?' are often followed up by more focused questions such as 'How can I involve weaker, more reluctant learners?' The outcomes of this type of exploration may trigger the teacher to think of ways in which interaction patterns can be used more effectively in class. This may lead to observing colleagues, reading articles or books, or simply trying out new ideas.

Other research instruments

Observation, questionnaires, and interviews have been identified as the main methods of enquiry, but of course there are other methods that teachers can use and combine. For example, it is possible to explore individuals' actions in more depth. These are often referred to as 'case studies'. By focusing on a group or an individual in more detail, teachers can track development over a period of time and gain more insights into the complexities of a specific case. Another option is to focus on teaching and learning materials. For example, a group of teachers may be interested in comparing new coursebooks to decide which one is most suitable, as suggested in Chapter 9. Teachers can also move beyond the physical boundaries of their own classrooms by, for example, interviewing other colleagues, parents, or administrators to find out their views on something relevant to teaching and learning.

Approaching the same question in different ways

When teachers wish to explore quite a broad question or issue, there may be several methods that they can choose from. It is important to think about the differences between methods with regard to the results they will show. For example, a teacher might have a discussion with colleagues about the impact of praising children frequently. She may be wondering whether she gives sufficient positive feedback to her children. If she wants evidence as to what is happening in her classroom in this respect, she could use a variety of instruments. The teacher could ask a colleague to observe her lessons and fill in a tick sheet. Alternatively, she could video or audio record her lesson to get linguistic evidence of how she uses feedback. Another idea would be to engage in systematic reflection (after every lesson) in diary writing and visiting other colleagues' lessons. Yet another would be to ask children in her classes about how they felt about feedback and praise. Each method would yield different data and would provide the teacher with different insights. This means that each of these instruments would actually answer a slightly different question about using praise and positive feedback. The tick sheet filled in by a colleague would give the list and frequency count of the various feedback phrases. The video or audio recording would also give a permanent record of the language the feedback was embedded in. It would be possible to engage in detailed analysis of the actual language use and the unfolding interaction around the feedback episodes. The video would also allow for the analysis of the teacher's and students' body language. The diary would give a record of the teacher's developing thinking about giving feedback and praise as a result of reflecting on the issue and picking up ideas from colleagues' classes. The data from children would give a sense of the effect of such feedback or the lack of it from the children's point of view. All of these are possible angles to start from. Which methodology to choose will depend on what aspect of the question the teacher is interested in.

Using more than one instrument

Gathering data from more than one source can provide teachers with more reliable results. This is often referred to as triangulating data. The word suggests that three angles are used to find answers to a question. For example, a colleague might observe something in a teacher's classroom; then the teacher may decide to record himself and finally ask the children's opinions on the same issue. This would mean that the same question or issue would be explored in more depth and any finding confirmed by all three instruments could be presented as convincing evidence. Arguably, the more we know about our learners, and about how they behave and react in various situations, the more we will be able to base our teaching decisions on realistic needs. For example, if a teacher is using questionnaires or interviews, it is advisable to combine these main instruments with some sort of observation. Another way in which teachers can get data about children is by asking parents. Parents are very important partners when it comes to a child's learning at school. They know their children best and therefore their input can be very valuable to teachers. Children may act very differently at home and at school. For example, many teachers have come across shy children who rarely initiate interactions in class or contribute spontaneously to activities. When teachers talk to parents they may discover that these children display their knowledge spontaneously in their home environment. Such discoveries will help teachers gain a better and more realistic understanding of these children's abilities. It is also important for teachers to encourage parents to help children with their English at home in a way that builds on what happens at school. Informing parents about the aims and expectations and the main principles of the approach teachers follow can be a very useful way of fostering positive relationships with enthusiastic parents who will then be ready to help with teachers' research.

Summary

Investigating classrooms, the learning process, and their own practices are part and parcel of effective teachers' practice. The more teachers know about the classroom complexities and the children they are working with, the better their chance for success. This chapter reviewed the basic principles of using child-friendly research instruments with children. Children's views and opinions should be valued and this is consistent with the principles advocated in this book.

Recommended reading

Background theory

Greig, A. and **J. Taylor.** 1999. *Doing Research with Children.* London: Sage Publications.

A comprehensive and practical introduction to undertaking research with child subjects. The book offers theories, frameworks, and some authentic research data from children. The unique nature of children as research subjects is emphasized.

Eder, D. and **L. Fingerson.** 2001. 'Interviewing children and adolescents' in J. B. Gubrium and J. A. Holstein (eds.): *Handbook of Interview Research.* Thousand Oaks, London: Sage Publications.

This article summarizes issues and problems that researchers face when working with child interviewees and offers creative solutions to some of these problems.

Lewis, A. 1992. 'Group child interviews as a research tool' *British Educational Research Journal* 18/4: 413–421.

This article offers a theoretical background to child interviews and a very practical step-by-step description of the child group interview.

Practical teacher resources

Wajnryb, R. 1992. *Classroom Observation Tasks: A Resource Book for Language Teachers and Trainers.* Cambridge: Cambridge University Press.

This book contains 35 structured tasks guiding teachers through the process of setting up classroom observations, conducting them, and analysing the data. This is an excellent resource for teams of teachers considering embarking on action research projects.

Tasks

If you would like to look at some practical tasks to explore your own practice related to the content of this chapter, you can try Tasks 6: Getting children to reflect on their learning (1), 7: Observing children working together (writing), 10: Observing children choosing tasks, 15: Observing other teachers' classes, 16: Keeping a teaching diary, and 17: Recording your own lessons (Appendix pages 159, 160, 163 and 165).

APPENDIX

EXPLORING YOUR OWN PRACTICE: SUGGESTED TASKS

This section of the book contains 17 practical tasks related to the content of the chapters in the book. Some tasks are relevant to the content of more than one chapter. The aim of these tasks is to encourage teachers to explore their own practice. Some tasks suggest observing children in different situations, others invite teachers to explore and record their own thinking and decisions or observe other teachers. Yet others suggest creating or adapting teaching/learning materials for their own contexts. The tasks may be useful for individual teachers, groups of teachers working in collaboration, or for teacher training sessions. The tasks can be used independently of the chapters of the book, too. Comments after tasks have been included (where appropriate) to indicate possible responses to texts, classroom extracts, and other materials used as prompts for discussion and exploration. This is not a complete list of tasks in any sense. Teachers and teacher trainers may want to use them as starting points for discussion or exploration or they may want to change or adapt them as they see fit for their contexts.

Task 1   Exploring different age groups

Do you teach different age groups? Think about the types of activities you use with different age groups. Look at the list of activities (on the next page) that might occur in English classes for children. Tick which age group in your context you think these activities would work with. Is it easy to decide? Can you add other activities that you use in your class?

Comments

It is often difficult to decide about these activities without any information about the context, the actual design features, or the way these activities are presented and implemented in class. However, it is possible to say that even the youngest children will enjoy joining in with stories or miming games

	Under eight years old	Over eight years old
1 A counting game which involves adding numbers up to 100 fast		
2 Listening to a story and joining in with repeated lines		
3 A gap task where two partners have to create a story together without looking at each other's pictures		
4 A gap-fill task where children have to complete sentences with one word		
5 A guessing game where children have to ask yes/no questions to find out what is in the teacher's bag		
6 A discussion task to debate in groups what present to buy from a limited budget for somebody's birthday in the class		
7 A miming game where children come forward and mime a spare time activity and the class try to guess the word		
8 A describe and draw task played in pairs		
9 Reading a short text and answering comprehension questions		
10 Writing a short paragraph about one's family		
Other tasks/activities		

whilst using gap tasks or participating in discussion tasks will be quite challenging for most ten- and 12- year-olds.

Task 2 Observing teachers' language use

Look at the following extract from an English lesson in Spain. How does this teacher build on the children's utterances in their first language? She is setting up a gap activity and gives all instructions in English to a beginners' class.

Teacher:	Right now. Listen, I will explain to you (touches her ear). Now you've got this and you've got this (leans forward, hands out black/white version of the picture to the As). Now Carlos and Bea, you've got a picture. It is a secret (whispers and holds the picture to her chest).
Child (1)	Que? (Pardon)
Teacher	Secret. Secret (whispers and holds the picture to her chest again).
Child (2)	Que no lo podemos ver. Y tenemos que adivinar que color es. (We can't look at it. We have to guess the colours.)
Teacher	Exactly. You (points to Carlos and Laura) have to say the colours that are here. So you say, for example, (holds out her hand with palm facing upwards) 'The banana is yellow' for example. And you colour it in (pretends to colour).
Child (2)	Ah, vale Bea. Que ellos dicen los colores y nosotros tenemos que pintar (Oh, right Bea. So they say the colours and we have to do the colouring).
Teacher	Exactly.

(data from Reilly 1994)

Comments

The teacher encourages the children to work out what they have to do by using lots of gestures and visual aids, and by demonstrating some of the actions herself. She is building on the children's instincts to work out the meanings and she gives positive feedback in the foreign language to children who are willing to contribute even if only in Spanish. It would probably be much quicker to explain in Spanish what the children should do but the teacher is investing effort and time into introducing the children to some useful language which will no doubt be recycled later as instructions for other similar games and activities. Such input is just at a level where the learners find they have to make an effort to understand the messages but they can do this with the help of the clues and support readily available from the environment.

Task 3   Exploring children's first language performances

Imagine that in your class you would like to try out a new pair or group task, for example, an 'information gap' task, a 'describe and draw' task, or a small group 'role-play'. Ask the children to do the tasks first in their own language and observe what difficulties, if any, they have. How can this exercise help you with your planning when it comes to setting up tasks and activities in English?

Task 4   Observing children outside English classes

Choose a group of learners where you are not the class teacher. Observe their classes in other subjects and take note of possible topic areas and projects that could be integrated into your English class. Discuss with the children what ideas they have.

Task 5   Exploring teaching and learning contexts

Think about your context. Make a list of all the advantages (such as good size classrooms, access to Internet, freedom to choose supplementary materials, co-operative colleagues) and the disadvantages (English lessons are restricted to just two hours a week, no English library at school, large classes). Do you make the most of your advantages? What is the best way to deal with the disadvantages? Could you turn any of them into opportunities for change? What else could you and your colleagues do to make the teaching/learning process more effective and enjoyable in your context?

Task 6 Getting children to reflect on their learning (1)

Design a role-play task which children can rehearse in pairs. Get them to record their performance and then let them practise a bit more and record their performances again. Let them listen to their own performances and discuss with you what changes they noticed and why. Talk about the importance of practice and repetition in learning. Some children may be interested in starting a homework tape where they can record themselves on speaking tasks at home either individually or with a friend or sibling.

Task 7 Observing children working together (writing)

Design some simple writing tasks such writing a card or a letter and get the children to work on them collaboratively, in pairs. Observe or record their conversations as they work together. How do they help each other? What can you learn from this?

Task 8 Exploring textbooks

Examine a coursebook that you are familiar with. What is the approach to vocabulary teaching? Choose a unit and check how and where the vocabulary taught gets recycled. Design an activity to recycle vocabulary from three units.

Task 9 Observing children working together (speaking)

Look at the data below. Two ten-year-old boys are interacting here using an information gap task. Both children have in front of them a picture of a house, and there are six differences between their pictures. The aim of the task is to find these differences without looking at each other's pictures. Can you see any problem with how they approach the task? How can the teacher help them?

L1   There are three flowers in the kitchen.
L2   There is a boy playing the guitar at the ground floor.
L1   Then, first xx I haven't got a guitar. There there are two cheeses in the kitchen.
L2   On the first floor there is a woman sleeping on a chair.
L1   There is a x there is a bird in the first, or um, first floor.
L2   I haven't got a bird in the first floor. In the bathroom there is a girl.
L1   Hm, hm, there is a there are two fishes in the bathroom.
L2   I have not got two fishes. I have just one, and that is the second.
L1   There are two apples in the kitchen.
L2   I have got four apples in the kitchen.
L1   The four, the, there is a dog in the second floor.
L2   I have not got a dog on the second floor. x There is a boy eating a sandwich on the second floor?

Comments

The children are describing their pictures very well but they do not seem to listen to or take notice of each other. They do not explicitly respond to each other with 'yes' or 'no' so it is impossible to know how many differences they think they found. The teacher might like to talk through the steps of carrying out this task more effectively, i.e. 'scaffold' them through the task. For example, the teacher might like to attract their attention to the fact that it is important to look for the differences in a systematic way, from left to right or from top to bottom. It is also important to listen carefully to what your partner is saying and clarify messages if in doubt at all.

Task 10 Observing children choosing tasks

Let children choose an activity that they enjoy doing in the last ten minutes of five or six consecutive lessons. Take note of what happens. Who selects what? Do they seem to be interested in their choice of activity? Who needs help? Who surprises you? Who changes their behaviour after the first few lessons?

Task 11 Getting children to reflect on their learning (2)

Before you start a new unit in the book, let children look through it and comment on the content. Ask them what they think the unit is about and what they think they are going to learn. Ask them what they think they will find easy or difficult and what they will enjoy. Would they like to add anything? Do similar reflections at the end of the unit. Repeat this with three or more units in the book and take note of the changes in their ability to reflect and respond.

Task 12 Planning lessons

Choose one of the topics of **Seasons**, **Holidays**, or **Sports** and brainstorm activities for one of your classes for three lessons.

Use a mind map and put your chosen topic in the middle of the circle. Try to organize the activities for the three lessons, sequencing the activities according to how difficult they are. Think about variety and logical progression. Decide on a main objective for each lesson and make sure there is a clear outcome for each lesson.

Lesson 1 Objective(s) Steps	**Lesson 2** Objective(s) Steps	**Lesson 3** Objective(s) Steps

Look at your overall plan for the three lessons. Is there anything missing? Does it look balanced in terms of variety of activities, skills, interaction patterns? If not, make some changes. Do the activities look engaging and motivating? If you get the chance, share your ideas with a colleague and then try them out with a group of learners. Write notes about how the lessons went. Is there anything to change/keep in mind for next time?

Task 13 Exploring authentic materials

These two popular poems were written for native speaker children of English. Would you be able to use them for one of your English classes? If yes, for what learning purpose(s)?

Cats

Cats sleep
Anywhere,
Any table,
Any chair,
Top of piano,
Window-ledge,
In the middle,
On the edge,
Open drawer,
Empty shoe,
Anybody's
Lap will do,
Fitted in a
Cardboard box,
In the cupboard
With your frocks –
Anywhere!
They don't care!
Cats sleep
Anywhere.

By Eleanor Farjeon

Mice

I think mice
Are rather nice

Their tails are long,
Their faces small,
They haven't any
Chins at all.
Their ears are pink,
Their teeth are white,
They run about
The house all night.
They nibble things
They shouldn't touch

> And no one seems
> To like them much.
>
> But I think mice
> Are nice
>
> *By Rose Fyleman*
>
> *(Both poems taken from Webb 1979)*

Comments

Both of these poems are excellent to introduce when children are learning about animals' habits or describing animals. The one about cats can be cut up and recreated in many different ways by moving the sections that rhyme forwards or backwards. For example, 'top of piano / window ledge / in the cupboard / on the edge' can be moved freely within the poem. Both poems are excellent for practising rhyming words and rhythm in English. Children might want to memorize them. They can also try to write simple poems (not necessarily with rhyming words) about other animals they like or pets they have.

Task 14 Designing your own learning materials (assessment tasks)

Examine a typical unit in your coursebook and design some assessment tasks to use at the end of the unit to discover what the children learnt. Consider more than one instrument.

Task 15 Observing other teachers' classes

These are classroom observation notes taken by a primary English teacher observing a colleague in a class teaching beginner six-year-old children in China. The purpose of the observation was professional development. These two teachers simply wanted to learn from each other. Look through the notes and think about what you can learn from this lesson. Do you think this teacher was happy with this class? What other activities could have been used to teach the same language to this class?

Classroom observation notes
Teacher's name: C.
Subject: English
Type of pupils: six-year-old first-year primary pupils in their second month of learning English: Number of pupils: 48

Level of the lesson: second month of learning English
Date: October 20, 1999
Lesson duration: 40 minutes
Observer: Z

Procedures:	Activities of the teacher and the pupils
Revision	Some words for family members (for example, grandfather, grandmother) and professionals (for example, doctor, farmer) learnt in the previous lessons were reviewed through pictures. The pictures were pasted on the blackboard with the corresponding words written under each of them. The words were again checked in the class. A recording was played, giving information about the jobs of each member of a family. The pupils were asked to match the family members to their respective jobs according to what they had heard from the tape.
Presentation of new words	The new words 'cook' and 'waiter' were presented by means of pictures. The pupils were asked to read after the teacher several times. Some pupils were asked to act out the two words. The pictures were pasted on the blackboard and the words were written under the corresponding pictures. Two other new words 'policeman' and 'postman' were presented and practised in the same way described above.
Practice of new words	The pupils were asked to point to the right picture corresponding to the word that the teacher pronounced. The pupils were asked to act out the word pronounced by the teacher. The pupils were asked to read all the words on the blackboard three times after the teacher. The pictures were pointed to one after another by the teacher, and the pupils were asked to say the right words. Some pupils were asked to come to the blackboard to read a word, with the rest of the class reading after him/her. The teacher said the words in Chinese, and the pupils were to respond in English. The pictures were rearranged on the blackboard into different places. The pupils were asked to match the words to the corresponding pictures.
Practise the pattern 'He/She's a …'.	**T** (Pointing to a picture) What's his/her job? **Ss** Postman. **T** Bob is a worker. Who is Bob? **S** A (nominated) pupil came to the blackboard and pointed to the corresponding picture and said: 'He is Bob'.

Procedures:	Activities of the teacher and the pupils
A guessing game	The pupils were provided with objects such as a hammer, a toy gun, and the like. Each time a student was nominated and he/she was to choose one object and act it out. The rest were supposed to come up with the word the student acted out.
Comments	

(Data from Wang, Q., a teacher educator/trainer at Beijing Normal University, China)

Comments

This seems like a very competent and well organized lesson where the children achieved the goals of learning and practising new vocabulary. It is good to use real objects to focus children's attention and to let them touch things as they learn new concepts. This teacher made sure that the children could practise the new words in many different ways, by pointing to cards, matching new words with Chinese equivalents, and acting words out in a guessing game. Perhaps it would have been possible to practise in groups and pairs to ensure wider participation by children.

Task 16 Keeping a teaching diary

Start a diary and once a week write down one thing that surprised you in class. It could be something that the children commented on or something that they really enjoyed despite what you expected, or any other question or issue. Check your notes at the end of the term. Do you notice any pattern in your observations? How can you use this reflection data for the benefit of your teaching?

Task 17 Recording your own lessons

Record one of your lessons and transcribe it or simply listen to it on the tape. Do you notice anything that you were not aware of doing or saying at the time? Can you learn anything from this exercise to inform your future teaching?

GLOSSARY

Analytical learning/learners Mature learners who are able to analyse and manipulate component parts of language and look at language in an abstract way.

Bottom-up processing Language learners often have to build up their understanding of listening or reading texts from constituent parts, e.g. recognizing an *-ing* ending tells you that the word you are looking at is a verb even if you do not know what it means.

Chunks Words, phrases in a text (spoken or written) that belong together, e.g. 'see you tomorrow'. Learning new language in chunks is easier than learning the constituent parts separately. Using chunks can make speakers' production faster.

Cognitive strategies Learning strategies related to memory and thinking such as rehearsal or memorization, e.g. to remember the names of the planets of the Solar System, learners can write the names down and read them again and again until they can remember all the names without looking at the paper.

Cumulative repetitive story A story that contains repetitive and highly predictable language that children can easily remember and join in with, e.g. 'Where are you going?' 'To see the queen.' This occurs in the story of Chicken Licken every time the chicken meets another animal.

English as a foreign language (EFL) English is learnt as a school subject in an environment where children do no have many opportunities to use the language outside the classroom, e.g. in countries like Japan or Italy.

English as a second language (ESL) English is integrated into the curriculum in an environment where children have many opportunities to use the language outside the classroom, e.g. children of other nationalities learning English in Australia or the USA.

Exposure to language All the language that children hear in and outside the school, e.g. listening to the teacher, watching television, listening to radio programmes, listening to children in the playground.

Global learners Learners who tend to want to understand the main ideas of a task or text rather than giving analytical attention to detail.

Holistic learning/learner Learners who are not yet able to analyse and manipulate language in an abstract way; they learn language by understanding meaningful messages. For example, in a song children will not understand every word but they will have an idea about what they are singing.

Immersion language environment A language environment where the learner has access to the target language outside the classroom and a real need to use the language; see also *ESL*.

Information gap An interactive activity where two children have different information on cards or pictures. They have to talk and complete the task without showing their information, cards, or pictures to each other, e.g. Spot the Differences task.

Integrated content and language A curriculum where different subject such as Science, Geography, and Maths are integrated with learning a second language. This is often referred to as the cross-curricular approach.

Kinaesthetic learner Learners who like to touch and feel things or move their bodies in expressive ways to aid their learning and communication.

Language modifications Alternative language forms used by speakers to achieve understanding or avoid misunderstanding in conversations, e.g. 'I said Alsatians, Alsatians are dogs, they look like wolves.'

Learning styles Learners' preferences with regard to their personalities and perceptual differences, e.g. a learner might be predominantly visual.

Learning to learn Fostering growing awareness about the learning process, e.g. how to monitor progress, how to plan, how to memorize new information.

Metacognitive strategies Learning strategies that help learners to plan, monitor, and evaluate their own learning. This is often referred to as the metacognitive cycle.

Metalinguistic awareness Learners' ability to reflect on language and language use, to be able to talk about language, e.g. knowing the labels 'nouns' and 'verbs'.

Multisensory teaching Teaching that takes into account children's perceptual differences and integrates colours, sound, movements, and touch into as much of everyday practice as possible.

Naturalistic language environment See *Immersion language environment*.

Rich language environment/input Language environment where learners have the opportunity to listen to and respond to a great variety of meaningful target language input.

Scaffolding An instructional strategy whereby the more knowledgeable partner (often parent or teacher) offers carefully adjusted support to help the child carry out a task so that the child can finally take over control of the task.

Top-down processing Language learners need to rely on their knowledge of the world and their predictions about content when they try to interpret reading and listening texts.

BIBLIOGRAPHY

Ahlberg, J. and **A. Ahlberg.** 1986. *The Jolly Postman.* London: Penguin Group.

Anderson, A. and **T. Lynch.** 1988. *Listening.* Oxford: Oxford University Press.

Batstone, R. 1994. *Grammar.* Oxford: Oxford University Press.

Berk, L. 2005. *Child Development.* Boston: Allyn and Bacon.

Biriotti, L. 1999. *Grammar is Fun: Young Pathfinder 8.* London: CILT.

Blondin, C., M. Candelier, P. Edelenbos, R. Johnstone, A. Kubanek-German, and **T. Taeschner.** 1998. *Foreign Language in Primary and Pre-school Education: a Review of Recent Research within the European Union.* London: CILT.

Bourke, K. 1999. *The Grammar Lab: Books 1–2.* Oxford: Oxford University Press.

Brewster, J., G. Ellis, and **D. Girard.** 2002. *The Primary English Teacher's Guide.* Harlow: Penguin English.

Bruner, J. S. and **A. Garton.** 1978. *Human Growth and Development.* Oxford: Clarendon Press

Burstall, C., M. Jamieson, S. Cohen, and **M. Hargreaves.** 1974. *Primary French in Balance.* Slough: NFER Publishing Company.

Bygate, M. 1987. *Speaking.* Oxford: Oxford University Press.

Cabrera, M. P. and **P. B. Martínez.** 2001. 'The effects of repetition, comprehension checks, and gestures, on primary school children in an EFL situation.' *ELT Journal* 55/3: 281–288.

Campbell, R. 2002. *Reading in the Early Years: Handbook.* (2nd edition). Buckingham: Open University Press.

Carpenter, K., N. Fujii, and **H. Kataoka.** 1995. 'An oral interview procedure for assessing second language abilities in children.' *Language Testing* 12/2: 157–181.

Chambers, G. and **D. Sugden.** 1994. 'Autonomous learning—the Danes vote yes!' *Language Learning Journal* 10: 48–57.

Chi, M. T. H. 1978. 'Knowledge structures and memory development' in R. S. Siegler (ed.): *Children's Thinking: What Develops?* Hillsdale, NJ: Lawrence Erlbaum.

Chomsky, N. 1965. *Aspects of the Theory of Syntax.* Cambridge, Mass: MIT Press.

Clark, M. 1990. *The Best of Aesop's Fables.* London: Walker Books Ltd.

Cohen, D. 2002. *How the Child's Mind Develops.* Hove: Routledge.

Cook, G. 2000. *Language Play, Language Learning.* Oxford: Oxford University Press.

Corden, R. 2000. *Literacy and Learning through Talk: Strategies for the Primary Classroom.* Buckingham: Open University Press.

Council of Europe. 2001. *Language Portfolios for Children.* London: Centre for Information on Language Teaching.

Cummins, J. 2000. *Language, Power and Pedagogy: Bilingual Children in the Crossfire.* Clevedon: Multilingual Matters.

Cunningham-Andersson, U. and **S. Andersson.** 1999. *Growing up with Two Languages: A Practical Guide.* London: Routledge.

Cunningsworth, A. 1995. *Choosing your Course Book.* Oxford: Macmillan.

Curtain, H. 2000. 'Time as a factor in early start programmes' in J. Moon and M. Nikolov (eds.): *Research into Teaching English to Young Learners.* Pécs (Hungary): Pécs University Press.

Dam, L. 1995. *Learner Autonomy 3: From Theory to Classroom Practice.* Dublin: Authentik.

Datta, M. and **C. Pomphrey.** 2004. *A World of Languages: Developing Children's Love of Languages: Young Pathfinder 2.* London: CILT.

Davies, P. A. 2002. *Zabadoo 3.* Oxford: Oxford University Press.

Donaldson, M. 1978. *Children's Minds.* London: Fontana Press.

Dörnyei, Z. 2001. *Motivational Strategies in the Language Classroom.* Cambridge: Cambridge University Press.

Doyé, P. 1999. *The Intercultural Dimension: Foreign Language Education in the Primary School.* Berlin: Cornelsen Verlag.

Dudeney, G. 2000. *The Internet and the Language Classroom.* Cambridge: Cambridge University Press.

Eder, D. and **L. Fingerson.** 2001. 'Interviewing children and adolescents' in J. B. Gubrium and J. A. Holstein (eds.): *Handbook of Interview Research.* Thousand Oaks, London: Sage Publications.

Ellis, G. and **J. Brewster.** 2002. *Tell it Again: The New Storytelling Handbook for Primary Teachers.* London: Longman.

Ellis, R. and **R. Heimbach.** 1997. 'Bugs and birds: children's acquisition of second language vocabulary through interactions.' *System* 25: 247–59.

Foster-Cohen, S. H. 1999. *An Introduction to Child Language Development.* London: Longman.

Gardner, H. 1983. *Frames of Mind: Theory of Multiple Intelligences.* New York: Basic Books.

Garvie, E. 1990. *Story as a Vehicle.* Clevedon: Multilingual Matters.

Geva, E. and **M. Wang.** 2001. 'The development of basic reading skills in children: a cross-language perspective.' *Annual Review of Applied Linguistics* 21: 182–204.

Gibbons, P. 1995. *Learning to Learn in a Second Language.* Merrickwill: Southwood Press Australia.

Gibbons, P. 2002. *Scaffolding Language, Scaffolding Learning: Teaching Second Language Learners in the Mainstream Classroom.* Portsmouth, NH: Heinemann.

Gilbert, I. 2003. *Essential Motivation in the Classroom.* London and New York: RoutledgeFalmer, Taylor and Francis Group.

Goto Butler, Y. 2004. 'What levels of English proficiency do elementary school teachers need to attain to teach EFL? Case studies from Korea, Taiwan, and Japan.' *TESOL Quarterly* 38/2: 245–278.

Gray, K. (ed.). 1996. *Jet Primary Teachers' Resource Book 1.* Surrey: Delta Publishing.

Greig, A. and **J. Taylor.** 1999. *Doing Research with Children.* London: Sage Publications.

Grieve, R. and **M. Hughes** (eds.). 1990. *Understanding Children.* Oxford: Oxford University Press.

Hasselgren, A. 2000. 'The assessment of the English ability of young learners in Norwegian schools: an innovative approach.' *Language Testing* 17/2: 261–277.

Herrera, M. and **T. Zanatta.** 2001a. *New English Parade Starter B.* Harlow: Pearson Education Limited.

Herrera, M. and **T. Zanatta.** 2001b. *New English Parade 6.* Harlow: Pearson Education Limited.

Hicks, D. and **A. Littlejohn.** 2002a. *Primary Colours Starter.* Cambridge: Cambridge University Press.

Hicks, D. and **A. Littlejohn.** 2002b. *Primary Colours 1.* Cambridge: Cambridge University Press.

Hicks, D. and **A. Littlejohn.** 2003. *Primary Colours 3.* Cambridge: Cambridge University Press.

House, S. and **K. Scott.** 2003a. *Story Magic 1.* Oxford: Macmillan Education.

House, S. and **K. Scott.** 2003b. *Story Magic 3.* Oxford: Macmillan Education.

Huang, J. 2003. 'Activities as a vehicle for linguistic and sociocultural knowledge at the elementary level.' *Language Teaching Research* 7/1: 3–33.

Ioannou-Georgiou, S. and **P. Pavlou.** 2003. *Assessing Young Learners.* (Resource Books for Teachers). Oxford: Oxford University Press.

Irujo, S. 1998. *Teaching Bilingual Children: A Teacher Resource Book.* London: Heinle & Heinle Publishers.

Kent, J. 1974. *The Fat Cat.* London: Puffin Books.

Kolsawalla, H. 1999. 'Teaching vocabulary through rhythmic refrains in stories' in S. Rixon (ed.): *Young Learners of English: Some Research Perspectives.* Harlow: Pearson Education Limited.

Kubanek-German, A. 2000. 'Early language programmes in Germany' in M. Nikolov and H. Curtain (eds.): *An Early Start: Young Learners and Modern Languages in Europe and Beyond.* Strasbourg: Council of Europe Publishing.

Lenneberg, E. H. 1967. *Biological Foundations of Language.* New York: Wiley.

Lewis, A. 1992. 'Group child interviews as a research tool.' *British Educational Research Journal* 18/4: 413–421.

Lewis, G. 2004. *The Internet and Young Learners.* (Resource Books for Teachers). Oxford: Oxford University Press.

Lightbown, **P. M.** and **N. Spada**. 2006. *How Languages are Learned.* (3rd edition). Oxford: Oxford University Press.

Lloyd, P. 1997. 'Children's communication' in R. Grieve and M. Hughes (eds.): *Understanding Children.* Oxford: Blackwell.

Long, M. 1983. 'Native speaker/non-native speaker conversation and negotiation of comprehensible input.' *Applied Linguistics* 4/2: 126–41.

Maidment, S. and **L. Roberts**. 2001. *Happy Street 2.* Oxford: Oxford University Press.

Marinova-Todd, S., D. Marshall, and **C. Snow**. 2000. 'Three misconceptions about age and L2 learning.' *TESOL Quarterly* 34/1: 9–34.

Martin, C. and **C. Cheater**. 1998. *Let's Join In! Rhymes, Poems and Songs: Young Pathfinder 6.* London: CILT.

McWilliams, N. 1998. *What's in a Word? Vocabulary Development in Multilingual Classrooms.* Wiltshire: The Cromwell Press.

Moon, J. 2000. *Children Learning English.* Oxford: Macmillan.

Nikolov, M. 1999. 'Why do you learn English? Because the teacher is short. A study of Hungarian children's foreign language learning motivation.' *Language Teaching Research* 3/1: 33–56.

Nikolov, M. and **H. Curtain** (eds.). 2000. *An Early Start: Young Learners and Modern Languages in Europe and Beyond.* Strasbourg: Council of Europe Publishing.

Oliver, R. 1998. 'Negotiation of meaning in child interactions.' *The Modern Language Journal* 82/3: 372–386.

Oliver, R., G. McKay, and **J. Rochecouste**. 2003. 'The acquisition of colloquial terms by Western Australian primary school children from non-English-speaking backgrounds.' *Journal of Multilingual and Multicultural Development* 24/5: 412–430.

Painter, L. 2003. *Homework.* (Resource Books for Teachers). Oxford: Oxford University Press.

Paran, A. and **E. Watts**. 2003. *Storytelling in ELT.* Whitstable, Kent: IATEFL.

Park, S. J. 2002. An Investigation into Korean Children's Perception of Key Variables that Influence their Language Learning. MA Dissertation, CELTE: University of Warwick.

Phillips, D., S. Burwood, and **H. Dunford**. 1999. *Projects with Young Learners.* (Resource Books for Teachers). Oxford: Oxford University Press.

Phillips, S. 1993. *Young Learners.* (Resource Books for Teachers). Oxford: Oxford University Press.

Piaget, J. 1923. *The Language and the Thought of the Child.* New York: Harcourt Brace and World.

Pinter, A. 2001. Explorations into Task-based Interaction with Non-proficient Young Learners of English. Unpublished PhD Thesis, University of Warwick.

Rea-Dickins, P. (ed.). 2000. *Assessing Young Language Learners.* Special issue of *Language Testing* 17/2.

Rea-Dickins, P. and **S. Rixon.** 1999. 'Assessment of young learners of English: reasons and means' in S. Rixon (ed.): *Young Learners of English: Some Research Perspectives.* Harlow: Pearson Education Limited.

Read, C. and **A. Soberon.** 2000. *Superworld 2.* Oxford: Macmillan Education.

Reilly, J. and **V. Reilly.** 2005. *Writing with Children.* (Resource Books for Teachers). Oxford: Oxford University Press.

Reilly, V. 1994. *A Study of Teachers' Paralinguistic Behaviour in Classes for Young Learners of English to Inform a Local Action Research Project about Useful Strategies in the Young Learners' Classroom.* MA Dissertation. CELTE: University of Warwick.

Reilly, V. and **S. M. Ward.** 1997. *Very Young Learners.* (Resource Books for Teachers). Oxford: Oxford University Press.

Revell, J., P. Seligson, and **J. Wright.** 1995. *Buzz 1 Teachers Book.* London: BBC English.

Rixon, S. 1993. *Tip Top 4.* London and Basingstoke: Macmillan Publishers.

Rixon, S. 1999. 'Where do words in EYL textbooks come from?' in S. Rixon (ed.): *Young Learners of English: Some Research Perspectives.* Harlow: Pearson Education Limited.

Rixon, S. 2000. 'Optimum age or optimum conditions? Issues related to the teaching of languages to primary age children' in *http://www.britishcouncil. org/english/eyl/articele01.htm.* British Council. Accessed 18 August 2005.

Romaine, S. 1995. *Bilingualism.* (2nd edition). Oxford: Blackwell.

Satchwell, P. 1997. *Keep Talking: Teaching in the Target Language: Young Pathfinder 4.* London: CILT.

Saunders, G. 1983. *Bilingual Children: Guidance for the Family.* Clevedon: Multilingual Matters.

Schneider, W. and **D. Bjorklund.** 1992. 'Expertise, aptitude and strategic remembering.' *Child Development* 63: 461–473.

Shak, J. 2005. *Friends: for Primary 5.* Professional Practice Project. CELTE: University of Warwick.

Singleton, D. 2001. 'Age and second language acquisition.' *Annual Review of Applied Linguistics* 21: 77–89.

Singleton, D. and **L. Ryan.** 2004. *Language Acquisition: The Age Factor.* (2nd edition).Clevedon: Multilingual Matters.

Skarbek, C. 1998. *First Steps to Reading and Writing: Young Pathfinder 5.* London: CILT.

Snow, C. 1972. 'Mothers' speech to children learning language.' *Child Development* 43: 549–65.

Stokic, L. and **J. Djigunovic.** 2000. 'Early foreign language education in Croatia' in M. Nikolov and H. Curtain (eds.): *An Early Start: Young Learners and Modern Languages in Europe and Beyond.* Strasbourg: Council of Europe Publishing.

Swain, M. 2000a. 'The output hypothesis and beyond: mediating acquisition through collaborative dialogue' in J. P. Lantolf (ed.): *Sociocultural Theory and Second Language Learning.* Oxford: Oxford University Press.

Swain, M. 2000b. 'French immersion research in Canada: Recent contributions to SLA and applied linguistics.' *Annual Review of Applied Linguistics* 20: 199–212.

Swain, M., and **S. Lapkin.** 1998. 'Interaction and second language learning: two adolescent French immersion students working together.' *The Modern Language Journal* 83: 320–38.

Thomsen, H. 2003. 'Scaffolding target language use' in D. Little, J. Ridley, and E. Ushioda (eds.): *Learner Autonomy in the Foreign Language Classroom: Teacher, Learner, Curriculum and Assessment.* Dublin: Authentik.

Thornbury, S. 1999. *How to Teach Grammar.* London: Longman.

Tierney, D. and **M. Hope.** 1998. *Making the Link: Relating Languages to Other Work in the School: Young Pathfinder 7.* London: CILT.

Tomlinson B. (ed.). 1998. *Materials Development in Language Teaching.* Cambridge: Cambridge University Press.

Tomlinson B. (ed.). 2003. *Developing Materials for Language Teachers.* London: Continuum Cromwell Press.

Tribble, C. 1996. *Writing.* Oxford: Oxford University Press.

Ushioda, E. 1996. *The Role of Motivation: Learner Autonomy 5.* Dublin: Authentik.

Vygotsky, L. 1978. *Mind and Society, the Development of Higher Mental Processes.* Cambridge, Mass.: Harvard University Press.

Wajnryb, R. 1992. *Classroom Observation Tasks: A Resource Book for Language Teachers and Trainers.* Cambridge: Cambridge University Press

Wallace, C. 1992. *Reading.* Oxford: Oxford University Press.

Webb, K. (ed.). 1979. *I like this Poem.* Harmondsworth: Penguin.

Wells, G. 1981. *Learning through Interaction: The Study of Language Development.* Cambridge: Cambridge University Press.

Wells, G. 1985. *Language, Learning and Education.* Windsor: NFER-Nelson Publishing Company Limited.

Wood, D. 1998. *How Children Think and Learn.* Oxford: Blackwell Publishers.

Wood, D., J. S. Bruner, and **G. Ross.** 1976. 'The role of tutoring in problem solving.' *Journal of Child Psychology and Psychiatry* 17: 89–100.

Wray, A. 2000. 'Formulaic sequences in second language teaching: principle and practice.' *Applied Linguistics* 21/4: 463–90.

Wright, A. 1997. *Creating Stories with Children.* (Resource Books for Teachers). Oxford: Oxford University Press.

Zanatta, T. and **M. Herrera.** 2000. *New English Parade 1, Teacher's Book.* Harlow: Pearson Education Ltd.

INDEX

References to the Glossary are indicated by 'g' after the page number.